Mastering Market Timing

Using the Works of L.M. Lowry and R.D. Wyckoff to Identify Key Market Turning Points

Richard A. Dickson
Tracy L. Knudsen, CMT

FT Press
Vice President, Publisher: Tim Moore
Associate Publisher and Director of Marketing: Amy Neidlinger
Executive Editor: Jim Boyd
Editorial Assistant: Pamela Boland
Senior Marketing Manager: Julie Phifer
Assistant Marketing Manager: Megan Colvin
Cover Designer: Chuti Prasertsith
Managing Editor: Kristy Hart
Senior Project Editor: Lori Lyons
Copy Editor: Language Logistics, LLC
Proofreader:Sheri Cain
Indexer: Erika Millen
Senior Compositor: Gloria Schurick
Manufacturing Buyer: Dan Uhrig

This book is sold with the understanding that neither the author nor the publisher is engaged in rendering legal, accounting, or other professional services or advice by publishing this book. Each individual situation is unique. Thus, if legal or financial advice or other expert assistance is required in a specific situation, the services of a competent professional should be sought to ensure that the situation has been evaluated carefully and appropriately. The author and the publisher disclaim any liability, loss, or risk resulting directly or indirectly, from the use or application of any of the contents of this book.

FT Press offers excellent discounts on this book when ordered in quantity for bulk purchases or special sales. For more information, please contact U.S. Corporate and Government Sales, 1-800-382-3419, corpsales@pearsontechgroup.com. For sales outside the U.S., please contact International Sales at international@pearson.com.

Company and product names mentioned herein are the trademarks or registered trademarks of their respective owners.

Printed in the United States of America
First Printing July 2011

Pearson Education LTD.
Pearson Education Australia PTY, Limited.
Pearson Education Singapore, Pte. Ltd.
Pearson Education North Asia, Ltd.
Pearson Education Canada, Ltd.
Pearson Educatión de Mexico, S.A. de C.V.
Pearson Education—Japan
Pearson Education Malaysia, Pte. Ltd.

Library of Congress Cataloging-in-Publication Data

Knudsen, Tracy L., 1968-
  Mastering market timing : using the works of L.M. Lowry and R.D. Wyckoff to identify key market
turning points / Tracy L. Knudsen, Richard A. Dickson,
     p. cm.
  ISBN 978-0-13-707930-8 (hbk. : alk. paper)
  1. Technical analysis (Investment analysis) 2. Wyckoff, Richard Demille, 1873-1935. 3. Lowry, L. M.
(Lyman M) I. Dickson, Richard A., 1948- II. Title.
  HG4529.K58 2012
  332.63'2042—dc22
                              2011012741
ISBN-10: 0-13-707930-3
ISBN-13: 978-0-13-707930-8

To my loving wife Sharon and to my girls,
Anne, Sara, and Jenn.
—Dick

To Carl and Jack:
My loving husband and precious son.
—Tracy

Contents at a Glance

Table of Contents

Acknowledgments

We would like to acknowledge Paul Desmond, President of Lowry Research Corp., for providing us with the support and resources necessary to complete this extensive project.

We also want to acknowledge Wyckoff expert Hank Pruden for his encouragement and support.

Finally, we would like to acknowledge Jim Boyd, Lori Lyons, and Gloria Schurick of Pearson for their help and patience throughout the publishing process.

About the Authors

Richard Dickson is a Senior Vice President at Lowry Research and Director of Research for the Domestic and Global versions of Lowry's primary product, Lowry on Demand. He also chairs the Research Committee for Lowry Capital Management. Dick has been a technical market analyst for more than 30 years. Prior to joining Lowry in 2002, Dick was Senior Technical Equity Strategist at two major regional brokerage firms.

Dick is a frequent contributor to many radio and television shows, and his words are seen often in newspaper and financial publications. Dick has served on the Board of Directors of the Market Technicians Association, first as Education Chair and later as Treasurer. He also served on the Board of Directors of the MTA Educational Foundation. In 1995, as head of the Market Technicians Association's Educational Committee, he initiated and taught the first full-credit course on technical analysis at the university level in the United States. In 1997, Dick received the MTA's "Best of the Best" award for his work in education. Dick is currently a member of AAPTA (the American Association of Professional Technical Analysts). He is a graduate of Principia College (BA) and the University of Virginia (MA).

Tracy Knudsen, Chartered Market Technician (CMT), has been a market technician for 17 years. She currently holds the positions of Senior Vice President of Research at Lowry Research Corporation and Assistant Portfolio Manager at Lowry Capital Management. Prior to joining Lowry's, Tracy held the position of Senior Market Strategist at Candlecharts.com and, prior to that, Senior Technical Analyst at Stone & McCarthy Research Associates.

Tracy has been quoted in major financial publications and written articles for the magazine *Stocks, Futures, and Options* as well as *Technical Analysis of Stocks and Commodities*. Tracy has also appeared on Bloomberg Radio's afternoon program, *Taking Stock*. Tracy is a member of both the Market Technicians Association and the American Association of Professional Technical Analysts, where she has served on the board of directors.

Foreword

The authors, Richard A. Dickson and Tracy L. Knudsen, deserve high-fives and extra kudos for making a significant and distinct contribution to the understanding and the application of the Wyckoff Method of technical market analysis. From their vantage points at Lowry Research, Dickson and Knudsen clearly and persuasively demonstrate the synergy gained through linking the principles of Richard D. Wyckoff with the research findings of L.M. Lowry. In this book, the authors show us how to use the Buying Power measure and the Selling Pressure indicator of Lowry Research to garner deeper, more accurate, and more relevant applications of Wyckoff's Law of Supply and Demand.

In my quest to understand the essence of Wyckoff, I frequently became stymied by the ambiguity of simple bar charts of price and volume when trying to decipher the relative impact of demand vs. supply in a given price action. But now, thanks to this book by Dickson and Knudsen, the separate measurements of demand and supply, using Lowry's indicators of Buying Power and Selling Pressure, offer the breakthrough I've needed. I now have the deeper, clearer, more efficacious grasp on the Wyckoff Method that I'd been seeking.

With clear-cut criteria and rich, understandable examples, Dickson and Knudsen whisk away the fog that surrounds simple bar chart analysis. They persuasively demonstrate how Lowry's indicators of Selling Pressure and Buying Power can help the analyst or the trader/investor to make timely and accurate judgments. They illustrate how to diagnose and then anticipate both the powerful bull market of the 1980s-90s and the devastating bear markets of the early 2000s. Dickson and Knudsen offer analyses of additional major bottoms and major tops to give the reader convincing evidence of the edge to be gained by uniting Lowry's Buying Power and Selling Pressure with Wyckoff principles.

As an additional bonus, the authors show how Wyckoff's Point-and-Figure Charts plus non-Wyckoff advance-decline indications are useful market tools for augmenting the Supply and Demand study of market tops and bottoms.

Finally, the reader can rely with great confidence upon both the technical competence and the personal integrity of Dick Dickson and Tracy Knudsen. I've been a professional colleague of Dick Dickson for numerous years. I was present in 1997 when Dick received from the Market Technicians Association (MTA) the well-deserved "Best of the Best" Award for his many accomplishments in technical market analysis education. In addition, I have had the pleasure of speaking with Tracy Knudsen at various Technical Analysis conferences throughout the country and can vouch for her knowledge and experience in the field of Technical Analysis. Prior to joining Lowry's, she was the Senior Technical Analyst at the highly respected firm, Stone and McCarthy Research, and then worked closely with noted Technician Steve Nison as Senior Market Strategist Candlecharts.com. I believe that this book, *Mastering Market Timing: Using the Works of L.M. Lowry and R.D. Wyckoff to Identify Key Market Turning Points*, is one of the high-point achievements of both their careers.

Henry O. (Hank) Pruden, PhD. Professor of Business and Executive Director of the Institute for Technical Market Analysis in The Ageno School of Business, Golden Gate University, San Francisco, CA U.S.A. Hank Pruden is author of *The Three Skills of Top Trading*, Wiley Press, 2007.

Introduction

Market timing doesn't work! At least that's what some people would like you to think. The Random Walk Theory and the efficient market hypothesis tell investors market timing is a fool's game. Academics have made careers out of ridiculing market timing. Mutual fund companies have issued hundreds, if not thousands, of reports deriding market timing while extolling "buy and hold," pointing out the investment disaster that awaits any investor who happens to miss the biggest up days in a bull market. (Curiously absent are similar reports about investment performance when missing the biggest down days.) Without a doubt, successful market timing is not easy. But it's not impossible, and when properly applied, market timing can generate big rewards for the time and effort expended.

We should emphasize that the equity market timing discussed in this book is not short-term in nature. No attempt is made to formulate short-term or day-trading timing strategies. The timing methods described in the following pages are aimed at the longer-term investor whose main interest is participating in the market's primary uptrends—bull markets—while avoiding the primary downtrends—bear markets. Thus, traders looking for systems detailing short-term entry and exit points for the market or for money-management techniques should seek advice elsewhere. Our intent is to provide investors with techniques for identifying major market tops and bottoms in the equity market based on the works of two masters of market analysis, Lyman M. Lowry and Richard D. Wyckoff.

Not all market cycles, though, are created equal in terms of benefiting from market timing. In a secular bull market, timing is of secondary importance to a buy and hold strategy, as the cyclical bear markets within the longer-term uptrend tend to be relatively shallow and short-lived. Make no mistake, successful timing will improve investment performance even within a secular bull trend. But timing becomes paramount during periods of secular bear markets. For instance, as of this writing, the S&P 500 Index is at the same level as in November 2004. In other words, an investment in a fund that tracks the S&P 500 would have resulted in no net gains, ex-dividends, over the past six years.

At this point, we should probably define what we mean by a secular bull market versus a secular bear market. First of all, what do we mean by "secular?" We don't mean temporal versus religious—although it could be argued some approach market analysis with religious fervor. We have to look all the way down to the third choice in the dictionary to find the applicable definition: "of or relating to a long term duration." Thus, we have the shorter term cyclical bull markets within a secular bear or a cyclical bear within a secular bull.

Now we have the definitions, but what are the characteristics that differentiate a secular market from a cyclical market? The key element differentiating a secular bull from secular bear is in the performance of the major price indexes themselves. In a secular bull market, bear markets tend to be short-lived, hence their characterization as "cyclical" bear markets. The lows in these bear markets also are far above previous bear market lows in the secular uptrend. For instance, the low in the 1984 bear market was well above the 1982 low, while the 1987 low was well above the '84 low, and so on. This is not true in a secular bear market. In the 1966–82 secular bear market, the 1970 low was well below the 1966 low, while the 1975 bottom was far below the 1970 low. See Figure I.1 for an illustration of these secular bull and secular bear patterns. In addition, the relative level of cyclical bear market lows appears to offer an early warning a secular bull is about to end. Although the 1942–1966 secular bull market did not top until 1966, the low in the 1962 bear market fell below the low of the 1960 bear—breaking a string of higher lows dating to 1946. Similarly, the March 2003 bear market low was below the low in the 1998 bear market (Figure I.2), breaking the string of higher lows in '84, '87, '90 and '98. This March '03 lower low plus the strong relative performances of new leaders in the energy, basic materials, and consumer cyclical stocks provided clear evidence the secular bull dating to the 1982 low had come to an end and signaled the start of a secular bear that, as of this writing, is still with us.

Note: You can access color versions of the illustrations on the book's website: www.ftpress.com/title/9780137079308.

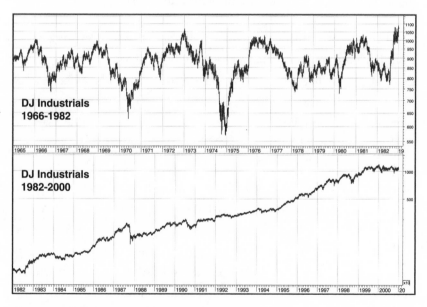

Charts created with Metastock, a Thomson Reuters product.

Figure I.1   DJIA Secular Bear Market 1966-1982 and Secular Bull Market 1982-2000

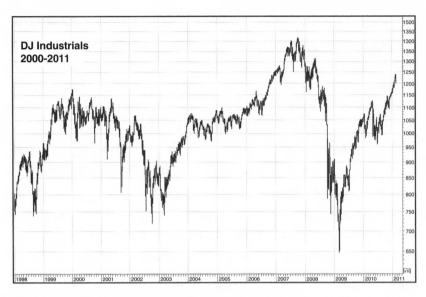

Charts created with Metastock, a Thomson Reuters product.

Figure I.2   Secular Bear Market 2000-2011 (thus far)

The emergence of new market leadership can be a key indication a shift from a secular bear to a secular bull (or vice versa) is taking place. For instance, the end of the 1966–1982 secular bear market was marked by a shift from stocks benefiting from inflation, such as metals (including gold), energy, and other commodity-based stocks, to those that would benefit from disinflation, such as consumer staples and finance stocks. The shift from the 1982–2000 secular bull market to a secular bear was marked by a similar shift away from technology and telecom stocks toward the basic materials, energy and consumer cyclical stocks that would lead in the 2003–2007 cyclical bull market. In both the 1982 and 2000 instances, the new leaders clearly outperformed the broad market indexes during the bear market, providing an early warning of a secular change in trend.

In addition to price, a second key element for identifying a secular bear market is the price/earnings ratio (or commonly referred to as the P/E ratio) for a major market index such as the S&P 500. The P/E ratio is based on the current price of the Index and, most frequently, the trailing 52-week combined earnings of the companies in the S&P 500. A secular bear market is characterized by a sustained contraction in the P/E Ratio, while in a secular bull market, the P/E Ratio shows a pattern of sustained expansion. Figure I.3 illustrates this pattern of contraction and expansion, using the inflation-adjusted average P/E Ratio for the S&P 500 on a rolling 10-year basis originated by Robert Shiller. As is evident, the P/E Ratio contracts steadily during the secular bear markets 1929-1948 and 1966-1982. In contrast, the Ratio expands during the secular bull markets 1948-1966 and 1982-2000. Based on these historic patterns, the sharp drop in the P/E Ratio since 2000 suggests the stock market is again in a secular bear trend.

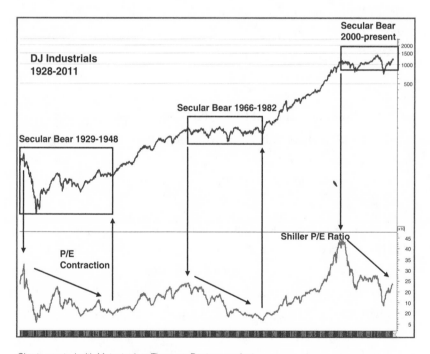

Charts created with Metastock, a Thomson Reuters product.

Figure I.3 S&P 500 Price/Earnings Ratio in Secular Bear Markets

To sum up, a secular bull market is characterized by steady, long-term uptrends in the major price indexes, interrupted from time to time by shallow and short-lived cyclical bear markets. A secular bear market is characterized by a series of bull and bear markets in which the major price indexes make little or no upside progress. This lack of progress was well-illustrated by the 1966–1982 bear market where the DJIA made an initial high just above 1000 in 1966 and then failed to exceed that high by an appreciable amount until November 1982. As noted earlier, a similar lack of progress is evident in today's market.

What does all this talk about secular bull and bear markets mean to an investor? In monetary terms, it means a lot. Despite all the ink spilled over the effects of missing x number of the biggest up days in a bull market, missing a bear market can be even more important for long-term investors. For example, in the 2007–2009 bear market, the S&P 500 suffered a drop of about 57%. This sickening drop was followed by an exhilarating rally of 80% in 2009–2010. Exhilarating, that is, for someone who had not just gone through the prior bear market. A hypothetical index fund investment of $100,000 at the market peak in 2007 would have dropped in value to just $43,000 by the time the S&P 500 bottomed out in March 2009. (For simplicity's sake, we're not factoring in dividends.) But what goes down comes back a lot slower because an 80% gain on $43,000 results in just $77,400, leaving our hypothetical investor still nearly $23,000 below his original $100,000. Ouch.

But, that's just one bear market. The longer-term impact of a secular bear market, which entails a number of cyclical bull and bear markets, can be even more dramatic. For example, the current secular bear market is presumed to have begun at the March 2000 market peak with the S&P 500 at 1527.35. Yet at the time of this writing, the S&P was at 1181, or nearly 23% *below* its 2000 peak. Thus, despite the 101% gain for the S&P 500 in the 2003–2007 bull market, and the Index's 80% gain in 2009–2010, our index fund investment would still be far below its value more than ten years before.

The secular bear market in place from 1966 to 1982, during which the DJIA (and S&P 500) failed to move appreciably above their 1966 highs tells a similar tale. In this case, we use the DJIA for our calculations, given that it was, at the time, the most widely followed index. From its 1966 high to its peak in 1981, the DJIA gained 2.9% (again, ignoring dividends). Thus, a $100,000 dollar investment would have appreciated to $102,900. Given the inflation of the late 1970s, it is likely an investor would have been less than impressed with this return, especially in terms of real (inflation-adjusted) dollars.

Historically, picking a bear market low or bull market high has been more associated with luck than with skill. But what if, through use of market timing, an investor was able to exit the market 10% below its bull market peak and then re-enter 20% above its bear market low? That's a substantial haircut from getting out at the top and in at the bottom. In this case, our hypothetical index fund investment of $100,000 at the 1966 high would have appreciated to $143,900 by the market high in 1981—not bad, considering the delayed exit and entry points. Using the methods developed by L.M. Lowry and Richard D. Wyckoff, though, it has been possible to identify the peaks and troughs of bull and bear markets much more accurately. In fact, using the entry and exit points based on the principles detailed in the following pages, our hypothetical 1966 $100,000 investment would have grown to $204,400 by the time the market peaked in 1981.

Let's be more specific here about the goals of this book. Richard D. Wyckoff (who you learn more about in the first chapter) identified specific market actions in terms of price and volume relationships, which he utilized, successfully, to identify turning points in equity price trends. A little later on, L.M. Lowry developed measures that quantify and display changes in the trends of Supply and Demand that are behind changes in equity price trends. Our aim is to enable an investor to recognize those actions that identify major changes in trend and to differentiate them from the day to day movements in the stock market. We do this by reviewing the major market tops and bottoms in the 1966–82 and 2000–present secular bear markets, identifying and explaining the key characteristics of each market action as it applies to the formation and conclusion of the major market tops and

bottoms. We then go on to identify and illustrate some other tools useful in recognizing major market tops and bottoms and continue with a
case study of the 2000–2001 market top (which was in many ways
unique) and conclude with a discussion of the current market.

The primary measures of the forces of Supply and Demand we
use along with the Wyckoff analysis are the Buying Power and Selling
Pressure Indexes, which form the basis of the Lowry analysis. Many
indicators have been developed to measure changes in Supply and
Demand, from On Balance Volume to various money flow and accu-
mulation/distribution indicators. However, Buying Power and Selling
Pressure are the only indicators of which we are aware to measure
changes in Supply and Demand independently, rather than plotting
changes as a single line. This allows for the application of the two
Indexes in analyzing the major trends of the stock market well
beyond their use in this book for identifying major tops and bottoms.
We realize Buying Power and Selling Pressure are propriety indicators to Lowry Research and, as such, available only to subscribers.
Nonetheless, we have found these indicators best complement the
Wyckoff analysis in measuring the forces of Supply and Demand at
major market tops and bottoms. Readers should note that the application of the Lowry indicators to the Wyckoff method is meant to
illustrate how the analyses of these two masters work together. It is
certainly possible to conduct an examination of major market tops
and bottoms on the basis of the Wyckoff analysis alone (which is
demonstrated in Chapter 9 through an analysis of the NASDAQ
Composite Index top in 2000). Readers interested in a more complete coverage of the Wyckoff analysis can contact the Wyckoff Stock
Market Institute in Phoenix, Arizona, which has available a study
course based on Mr. Wyckoff's original correspondence course introduced in the early 1930s.

Part I_____

A Wyckoff-Lowry Analysis of Major Market Tops and Bottoms Since 1968

In Part I, the authors examine the major market tops and bottoms in the secular bear markets from 1966-1982 and 2000-present, utilizing a detailed Wyckoff/Lowry analysis. The Wyckoff and Lowry methods are combined in an examination of the forces of Supply and Demand as they relate to the formation of bull market tops and bear market bottoms.

1 ————————————

Richard D. Wyckoff and
Lyman M. Lowry:
The Analysts and Their Methods

Richard D. Wyckoff

The technical approach to investment analysis dates back decades, if not centuries. In contrast to the fundamental approach to market analysis, which focuses on identifying the intrinsic value of a company and its future growth potential by utilizing such metrics as earnings, debt, and management prowess, technical analysis focuses largely on the study of price action. Technicians work under the assumption that security prices move in trends. The identification of those trends, in turn, can be used to forecast future price action. Early pioneers in the field of technical analysis include some well-known names such as Charles H. Dow, Ralph N. Elliott and William D. Gann. Perhaps lesser known are technicians Richard D. Wyckoff and Lyman M. Lowry. While icons in their own right regarding their contributions to the field of technical analysis, various writings on these two individuals indicate they were both very much students of the market. Another common thread between these two technicians was that both regarded the basic Law of Supply and Demand as the key element in their approaches to the analysis of stock market trends.

Richard D. Wyckoff began his career in 1888 as a stock runner at the young age of 15. By the age of 25, he had gained enough hands-on market experience to open his own brokerage office. From his perspective as a broker, Wyckoff was able to view the buying and selling patterns of the large market players. By doing this, he "realized it was possible to judge the future course of the market by its own action...that the action of stocks reflected the plans and purposes of those who dominated them...that the basic Law of Supply and Demand governed all price changes...that the best indicator of the future course of the market was the relation of Supply and Demand."[1] It was on this foundation, the Law of Supply and Demand, that Wyckoff based his method of forecasting the future direction of the market.

Wyckoff enjoyed great success in his forecasting technique and, as a service to his clients, published *The Ticker Magazine*. This publication's name was later changed to *The Magazine of Wall Street*, and Wyckoff's superior analytical and predictive abilities resulted in the largest circulation of any financial publication in the world at the time. In 1928, Wyckoff turned his business over to associates and, in 1931, his method of stock market analysis was published as a correspondence course. Wyckoff deemed this course "the cream of what I have learned in 40 years of active experience on Wall Street."[2] This course remains in existence today through the Stock Market Institute, based in Phoenix, Arizona.[3] The foundation of this course is the same now as it was in the 1930s, and that foundation is the Law of Supply and Demand.

Lyman M. Lowry

Lyman M. Lowry majored in Finance at the University of Nebraska, and his first taste of the stock market came in 1925 as a junior trust officer in a Florida bank. Initially, Lowry adopted the existing investment philosophy of the bank, which relied almost exclusively on the "fundamentals" and the news developments of the day. However, as the 1929 stock market crash unfolded, he quickly became disenchanted with portfolio managers who, frozen with fear, comforted each other with assurances that they owned nothing but high quality stocks, rather than preserve what was left of their customers' capital. Dissatisfied with the results of relying largely on fundamental analysis, Lowry left the bank in 1933 in favor of independent research.

He felt that there must be a way to analyze the condition of the market itself, rather than attempting to analyze the conditions surrounding the market. His search for a better method of analyzing the market led him to the Dow Theory. His enthusiasm for the Dow Theory was initially positive. However, he eventually found that even the so-called experts often disagreed at major turning points in the market. His conclusion was, "If the experts can't agree, what chance have I got of coming up with the right interpretation?"

Again disillusioned, Lowry undertook his own research of the stock market. Having majored in Finance, Lowry was well aware the first chapter of nearly every basic textbook on the subject of macro economics discusses the importance of the Law of Supply and Demand. And yet Lowry could see no evidence of this principle being used in the analysis of the stock market. It was his conviction that market trends override fundamentals and that the trends were ultimately the product of the basic Law of Supply and Demand. Thus it followed that, regardless of the reasons why, if the desire to buy is stronger than the desire to sell in any given period, prices automatically rise. And if the pressure to sell exceeds the desire to buy, prices automatically decline. It was as simple as that.

However, another important question needed answering. How do stocks reflect an over-balance of buyers in one period and an over-balance of sellers in another? With this question in mind, he set out to determine a method to measure Supply and Demand as it applies to individual stocks and the equity market in general. In the end, Lowry concluded that it all came down to price and volume. If a stock ends the trading day at a price above its previous close, it seemed reasonable to assume that it was purchased with more enthusiasm than with which it was sold. And given that the desire to buy or sell can also be measured in terms of activity, the volume of trading should be a prime consideration. Thus the action of the entire market, encompassing the individual actions of insiders, specialists, tape readers, fundamentalists and all other investors, could be reduced to simply four basic components: (1) Total gains for all stocks closing higher than the previous day's close; (2) the total volume of trading in stocks registering gains; (3) total losses for stocks closing lower than the previous day's close, and; (4) the total volume of trading for declining stocks.

Using data from the *Wall Street Journal* back to January 1933, Lowry calculated these metrics for each stock traded on the NYSE. It was an enormous effort given the fact that in those days there were no computers or databases, just hand-cranked adding machines.[4] Upon compiling the data, Lowry then began a series of exhaustive tests of various moving averages from 3 to 180 days run singly and in various combinations, to find the optimum way of using the data to portray Supply and Demand and measure market trends. "The studies made so much sense to me that I figured they would also be of interest to any serious student of the market." Thus with Mansfield Mills, an old friend with vast advertising and business experience, the firm Lowry and Mills was established at 40 Wall Street, New York City, in April 1938. To this day, nearly 80 years later, Lowry Research Corporation publishes the original indicators developed by Mr. Lowry from its offices in Palm Beach Gardens, Florida.

The Wyckoff and Lowry Methodologies: A More In-Depth Look

Richard D. Wyckoff, in his studies, set out to dispel the common belief that the stock market is a complex machine. This perception of complexity largely evolves from fundamental analysis, which requires the deciphering of dense and often verbose earnings and annual reports, among other things, in order to assess the probable fair value of a company. In contrast, technical analysis, the Wyckoff and Lowry Methods in particular, uses readily available data of a stock's own price action and volume to form logical assessments of market conditions.

The Wyckoff Method

The foundation of the Wyckoff Method of stock market analysis consists of three basic principles: The Law of Supply and Demand, The Law of Cause and Effect, and The Law of Effort vs. Result. It is a common misconception that because for every buyer in the market there is a seller, the Law of Supply and Demand does not apply to equities. To the contrary, the buyer and seller involved in every trade have different objectives, thereby causing Supply/Demand imbalances. For example, if an investor is holding shares of stock and wants to sell them, and is willing to accept a price lower than a previous seller of the stock in question, the price will fall. Simply stated, when Supply is greater than Demand, prices will fall, and when Demand is greater than Supply, prices will rise. The Supply/Demand relationship can be monitored by watching price and volume using a simple bar chart.

The Law of Cause and Effect deals with determining the degree or "effect" of an upcoming price move based on prior price action termed the "cause." For an effort to manifest itself in the form of a change in price, there must first be a cause. The Law of Cause and Effect moves hand-in-hand with the Law of Supply and Demand, with Demand representing a period of accumulation within a trading range and Supply representing a period of distribution over a similar period of consolidation. The effect realized by a cause, or period of accumulation or distribution, will be in direct proportion to that cause. Point and figure chart counts are used in the Wyckoff Analysis to measure a cause and project the likely extent of the subsequent effect.[5]

The Law of Effort vs. Result brings volume into the analysis process. Although price is often thought to be the key component in technical analysis, the volume behind price action is just as, if not more, important than the price action itself. Divergences between price action and volume often signal trouble. Specifically, when the amount of effort (volume) and extent of the result (price action) are not in sync, positions should be protected against a potential reversal of trend.[6]

Using a combination of these three basic principles, various
stages of the formation of major market tops and major market bottoms can be identified, with the objective to allow the investor to
enter the market in early stages of an important move higher or exit
the market and perhaps enter the short side in the early stages of a
major market decline. By capturing the "meat" of major market trend
and exploiting the direction of that trend, investors can reap superior
returns in their investment portfolios.

The Lowry Analysis

Few investors ever buy or sell a stock because of what they know
about it. It is what they think will happen to it that causes them to act.
Traders and investors are constantly trying to anticipate and discount
the future with the objective of realizing profits at some later date.
Their conclusions could be based on many factors including esti-
mated earnings, taxes, interest rates, inflation, news events, economic
conditions, or just plain hunches. The end result is that some buy,
thinking the stock price will advance. Others sell, believing prices will
be lower in the course of time. Some will be right, and some will be
wrong because the market trend cannot simultaneously proceed in
both directions. In the final analysis, the market can only be expected
to move in the direction of the greatest money influence.[7]

It has already been noted that the relationship between the total
buying desire and the total selling desire determines the direction of
the trend, and these two desires can be factually measured using four
basic calculations:

- Total point gains for stocks closing higher on the day
- Total volume for all stocks closing higher on the day
- Total point losses for all stocks closing lower on the day
- Total volume for all stocks closing lower on the day

These four essential tabulations, which are factual and unbiased,
provide the statistical foundation for the Lowry Analysis. These

metrics are also the foundation for the two indicators Lowry Research Corporation is most known for, the Buying Power and Selling Pressure Indexes. It is the trends of these two indicators that help determine the intermediate-term trend of the broad market.

Buying Power is an intermediate to longer-term measurement of the effect buyers are producing (Demand), as evidenced by the gains and volume registered by advancing stocks. Buying Power is a multiple-time-period index which, in its final construction, not only takes into account the number of stocks registering advances, but includes and evaluates such upside action both in terms of actual points gained and related upside volume. The average time period for its several components is approximately 50 trading days. Selling Pressure is Lowry's principal measure of the intermediate to longer-term trend of the force of Supply. It is computed in the same manner as the Buying Power Index but is constructed from the actions of declining stocks in terms of points lost and downside volume.[8]

The Buying Power and Selling Pressure Indexes act as leading indicators for the actions of the broad market, and the trends of these indicators can be used to identify the various stages of bull and bear markets. For example, in the strongest stage of a bull market, Buying Power will steadily rise while Selling Pressure steadily falls. Then, as the uptrend enters its latter stages, Selling Pressure will establish an uptrend, reflecting the increased profit taking that tends to occur as a bull market matures and a major topping formation begins. As the major top forms, the uptrend in Selling Pressure will eventually be joined by a turn lower in Buying Power, reflecting distribution and a lack of Demand typically seen in the early stage of a new bear market. Finally, as the bear market nears completion, the upward trend in Selling Pressure will start to wane and fail to confirm lows in the market itself, implying that the desire to sell is becoming exhausted.

In the chapters that follow, the melding of the Wyckoff and Lowry methodologies to identify major market bottoms and major market tops is presented using numerous examples dating as far back as 1966. Some supplementary indicators are also presented in the analysis in an effort to refine even further the ability to identify major market trends and turning points.

Endnotes

[1]   Jack K. Hutson, David H. Weis, Craig F. Schroeder, *Charting the Stock Market, The Wyckoff Method* (Seattle, WA: 1986), 4.

[2]   Hutson, 4.

[3]   http://www.wyckoffstockmarketinstitute.com/.

[4]   Chris Wilkinson, *Technically Speaking* (Greenville, SC: 1997), 145.

[5]   Hank Pruden, *The Three Skills of Top Trading* (Hoboken, NJ: 2007), 132.

[6]   Richard D. Wyckoff, Course in Stock Market Science and Technique; Introduction to the Wyckoff Method of Stock Market Analysis, Volume One, Text; The Stock Market Institute; (Phoenix, AZ: 1983) pg. 5.

[7]   Lowry Market Analysis Manual, Section 1–3 (North Palm Beach, FL: 2007).

[8]   Lowry Market Analysis Manual, Section 1–7 (North Palm Beach, FL: 2007).

2

How Major Market Tops Form: Part I, The Preliminaries

As any investor knows, most investment advice is focused on how to make money. We've all seen the advertisements promising to guide you on your path to financial wealth and freedom. Less acknowledged is the concept that not losing money can be just as important, if not more so, than making money in achieving a long-term goal of financial freedom. This is especially true during uncertain periods in the stock market.

As pointed out in this book's Introduction, between 1966 and 1982, the Dow Jones Industrial Average (DJIA) failed to achieve any meaningful gains above its level in early 1966. Despite the lack of overall gain, the DJIA still enjoyed several significant bull markets over this 16-year period—bull markets that afforded ample money-making opportunities. The key, however, was to not give back those bull market gains during the intervening bear trends.

Today, the stock market again appears mired in an uncertain period in which the major price indexes are making little headway over the long term. In fact, as of this writing, the DJIA is at a level first reached in early 1999, while the S&P 500 is at a level first achieved in early 1998. But since 1998–1999, there have been two bear markets, 2000–2003 and 2007–2009, in which the DJIA lost 37% and 54%, respectively. There has been one completed bull market, 2003–2007, in which the DJIA gained 94% and one ongoing bull market beginning in 2009, showing a gain in the DJIA, thus far, of 71%.

Because a 100% gain is needed to recoup a 50% loss, it's easy to see how avoiding these bear markets, while participating in the bull markets, can significantly improve investment performance.

The first step in avoiding a bear market is learning to identify a major market top. Note, this process is in no way an attempt at forecasting prices. Rather, it is the identification of characteristics that have been repeated time and again as a bull market transitions into a bear market. Although no two major market tops are identical, they all share common characteristics. But before a market top can form, there has to be a prior long-term uptrend.

The Life Cycle of a Market Uptrend (a.k.a. a Bull Market)

By the end of a bear market, prices have been driven low enough to the point where supply has been virtually exhausted, and buyers begin to snap up stocks at what they regard as long-term bargain prices. Buying at a true long-term bottom is done primarily by investors who see long-term appreciation potential in stock prices. However, market bottoms generated by traders tend to be temporary, as these buyers will typically sell their stocks after a short-term gain.

This first stage of a new bull market is termed the *accumulation phase*. Then as prices begin to rise, the new uptrend enters the markup phase. At this point, there is still a healthy dose of skepticism the stock market has entered a long-term uptrend. But demand is clearly dominant over supply as buyers are willing to pay higher prices in hopes of selling at still higher prices. (It has been said that Wall Street is one of the few places where higher prices beget still higher prices). Rising prices during this phase of the uptrend are also characterized as "climbing a wall of worry," reflecting the skepticism about the durability of the rally. Over time and as prices move steadily higher, this skepticism fades and is replaced by a conviction that the market has nowhere to go but up. This optimism leads to the next and final stage of the uptrend, known as the distribution phase.

The *distribution phase* can be described as a greedy place, as the dominant characteristic of the distribution phase is investor greed, where caution is generally thrown to the wind. Expectations are the party will never end, and prices will continue to climb ever higher. Even if prices do turn lower, the general consensus is there will be plenty of time to book profits before a new bear trend begins. Such optimism seems well-justified by equally optimistic reports about the economy and corporate earnings. But it is at this point those investors who scooped up stocks at bargain prices during the first phase of the bull market begin to unload their positions. The recipients of these unloaded stock positions are typically late-to-the-party buyers in a process known as the distribution of stock from strong hands (the early buyers) to weak hands (late buyers). Because these late buyers are purchasing stock at already-elevated prices, they are subject to almost immediate losses on any market pullback—hence the term weak hands. For example, had an investor bought XYZ at $10 early in the bull market and it rallied to $50, the stock could pull back to $40 and do little damage to the profit. But compare this to a buyer at $45 who would have almost an immediate loss once the stock began to decline. Consequently, this process of distribution is key to identifying a major market top. But how?

Characteristics of a Major Market Top

Richard Wyckoff was one of the first stock market analysts to recognize bull market tops tend to follow similar patterns of distribution. He also recognized market tops share common characteristics, reflecting the process by which supply overcomes demand. Subsequently, L.M. Lowry, writing in the late 1930s, devised a method of quantifying changes in the longer term trends of Supply and

Demand. Taken together, the Wyckoff and Lowry analyses provide powerful tools for identifying major market tops and bottoms.

Idealized Major Market Topping Pattern

While acknowledging that no two major market tops are identical, Richard Wyckoff identified what he believed are two phases common to all tops. The first phase is the distribution of stock from strong to weak hands. The second phase is the dominance of supply over demand, leading to the final collapse of the bull market into a new bear trend. This chapter deals with the distribution phase, and the next chapter details the terminal stage of a bull market and start of a new bear trend. The idealized characteristics of the distribution phase and end of a bull market as defined by Wyckoff are shown in Figure 2.1.

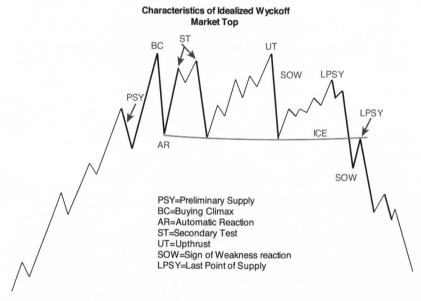

Figure 2.1   Wyckoff's key points for identifying a major market top

The first point of reference is termed *Preliminary Supply* (PSY). Prior to this, prices have been moving higher easily. The first sign of an approaching PSY is that prices begin to move higher in smaller amounts but with no significant drop in volume. This resistance to moving higher suggests the demand driving prices higher is beginning to meet more significant supply. Often, this resistance is accompanied by evidence of more selective buying interest. This selective buying is often reflected by lagging breadth as seen in a broad-based advance-decline line, such as the one for stocks traded on the New York Stock Exchange (NYSE). PSY itself is characterized by a heavy volume pullback, frequently the heaviest volume pullback thus far in the uptrend. This is the first indication of aggressive distribution, as long term investors begin to unload positions bought at much lower prices. However, this pullback is typically seen as an opportunity to buy stocks at better prices by those coming late to the rally. This new demand limits the downside in the PSY to an apparently normal correction in the market's primary uptrend.

As prices recover from the PSY and resume their move higher, buyers begin to panic into stocks, fearing they will miss the next big rally. This panic buying produces the next phase of the topping pattern, the Buying Climax (BC on Figure 2.1). The Buying Climax is typically a one or two-day affair and is characterized by extremely heavy volume. The surge higher, though, cannot be maintained, as the spike in prices motivates earlier buyers to aggressively dump their stocks on the market. The result is an initial spike higher but a close near the low for the day (or for a 2-day BC, the low is recorded on the second day). Typically, the Buying Climax marks the final exhaustion of strong demand in a bull market. From this point on in the topping process demand tends to be of poor quality. That is, most stock is now held by weak hands—those who bought late in the bull market. In contrast supply is of good quality, that is, willing sellers who bought at substantially lower prices and who can still sell at significant profits.

As wary buyers move to the sidelines and sellers step in, the Buying Climax is typically followed by a decline, termed by Wyckoff as the Automatic Reaction (AR on Figure 2.1). Sellers are now active, so volume can remain relatively heavy on this decline. The bottom of this Automatic Reaction often serves to define the lower limit of the trading range that defines price movement as the topping process progresses. The Automatic Reaction also typically marks the start of active distribution. At this point, however, not all late buyers have abandoned hope for higher prices. Rather, they see the pullback on the Automatic Reaction as a temporary pause in an ongoing bull market and as another opportunity to buy at lower prices. The rally that results from these bargain hunters' activities is termed the Secondary Test (ST).

The primary role of the Secondary Test is to help determine the balance of Supply and Demand. If demand remains strong, then the Secondary Test rally will surpass the top of the Buying Climax. In this case, volume is usually heavy on the rebound. A failed test, however, will likely be accompanied by weak or falling volume and a shrinking range between the daily intraday highs and lows. The initial Secondary Test typically defines the upper limit of the topping formation and is followed in the succeeding days and weeks by a series of rallies and reactions as the process of distribution continues. The end of this distribution process is marked by signs buyers have stepped aside (demand has been exhausted) and sellers have become the dominant players in determining the market's trend. The end of the distribution process is discussed in the next chapter, which covers the final stages of a major market top.

Lowry Indicators

While the Wyckoff analysis of market tops may seem cut and dried, there can be instances when the patterns of price and volume lack clarity. This is where utilizing the tools offered by the Lowry analysis can shed light and help validate the Wyckoff patterns. In analyzing market tops, there are three primary tools used by the Lowry analysis: 90% Days and, most importantly, the Lowry Buying Power and Selling Pressure Indexes.

As will be explained in Chapter 4, "How Major Market Bottoms Form: Part 1, Panic & Capitulation," the concept of 90% Days was first introduced by the current principal at Lowry Research, Paul Desmond, in 1982. The rationale for 90% Days is they represent severe imbalances between Supply and Demand. Thus an imbalance in demand could be reflected by panic buying in a 90% Up Day. Likewise, an imbalance in supply reflects panic selling in a 90% Down Day. The calculation for a 90% Day entails both Up and Down Volume plus Points Gained and Points Lost, all of which are the essential elements in measuring Supply and Demand. Up Volume is simply the total volume of all stocks on the NYSE advancing for a day's session. Down Volume is the total volume for all the NYSE stocks declining for the day. Points Gained is the cumulative total points for all advancing stocks in a day's trading, while Points Lost is the cumulative total points for all declining stocks. A 90% Up Day, therefore, occurs when Up Volume is 90% or more of the trading session's total Up plus Down Volume and Points Gained is 90% or more of the total Points Gained plus Points Lost for the session. Similarly, a 90% Down Day occurs when Down Volume is 90% or more of the session's total Up/Down Volume and Points Lost is 90% or more of the total Points Gained/Points Lost. Variations of the 90% Day concept have appeared over the years, most often based only on Up/Down Volume. However, to qualify as a true 90% Day, both Points and Volume must be included. As an advertisement might state..."accept no substitutes."

The Law of Supply and Demand is the bedrock for all analysis at Lowry Research. The principal means for measuring the forces of Supply and Demand are the Selling Pressure and Buying Power Indexes. First introduced by L.M. Lowry in the late 1930s, the Buying

Power and Selling Pressure Indexes are tools for measuring the inter-mediate to longer-term trends of Supply and Demand. Although the calculation is proprietary, these Indexes include daily Up/Down Volume, total Volume, Points Gained and Points Lost. Volume figures are based on Composite NY Stock Exchange figures. Expanding or con-tracting demand is reflected by sustained uptrends or downtrends in Buying Power. Similarly, increasing supply is indicated by an uptrend in Selling Pressure, while a downtrend reflects contracting supply. The strongest market uptrends are accompanied by an uptrend in Buying Power and downtrend in Selling Pressure.

As a bull market matures, profit-taking begins to increase. As a result, it is not uncommon to see both Buying Power and Selling Pressure rising in the latter stage of a bull market. Supply begins to expand on more widespread profit-taking while continued strong fun-damental factors (such as rising earnings and a strong economy) fuel continued demand. In the final stages of a bull market, though, it is the action of Selling Pressure that moves to the forefront, as it best illustrates the process of distribution that occurs at major market tops.

Combining the Wyckoff and Lowry Analyses in Identifying Major Market Tops

Although 90% Days are key factors in identifying major market bottoms, they are relatively minor factors at major market tops. When found, 90% Down Days most frequently occur at the time of PSY and act as confirming evidence of the heavy selling that normally marks this pattern. In general, though, 90% Days were relatively rare at major market tops, at least until 2007 when the abolition of the Up-Tick Rule helped fuel a proliferation of both 90% Up and Down Days.

Contrary to the limited appearance of 90% Days at market tops, the Buying Power and, especially, Selling Pressure Indexes are very useful tools in helping identify the various Wyckoff elements of a market top. For instance, at PSY, Selling Pressure will quite often show a sharp spike higher, underlining the surge in supply that identifies this pattern. The Selling Pressure Index can also be useful in highlighting a continued pattern of distribution as prices rise and fall in Secondary Tests and Automatic Reactions as the topping process progresses. A sustained rise in Selling Pressure can be especially useful during these tests of the market's high, as price alone can be a misleading indicator of market strength. At the same time, a flat to lower trend in Buying Power during Secondary Test rallies suggests a pattern of contracting Demand. In turn, this suggests a market with insufficient strength to renew the bull trend. Taken together, the Buying Power and Selling Pressure indexes are important elements in helping identify the shift in control from buyers to sellers that is part of every major market top.

All this theory is well and good, but how do the Wyckoff and Lowry analytical techniques hold up during actual market tops? For an answer, we turn to an examination of the major market tops during the secular bear market 1966–82 and then to the 2007 top in what many perceive as the current-day secular bear market.

The Top of the 1966–1969 Bull Market

After a 9-month bear market that began in early 1966, the DJIA started a new bull run in October 1966. The bull market was interrupted by a nearly 10% pullback lasting from September 1967 to March 1968, after which the DJIA again turned higher. As seen in Figure 2.2, this rally peaked in early May and was followed by a two-month trading range, after which the DJIA fell to a reaction low in August. From this reaction low, the stock market enjoyed a virtually uninterrupted advance over the next two months that carried the DJIA to a new rally high for the bull market by mid-October. At this point, though, the rally suffered a significant hiccup in the form of a sharp two-week setback that occurred on volume equal to the heaviest seen during the rally from the August low. This heavy volume suggested a potential point of Preliminary Supply (PSY) had been reached. The potential for a PSY was supported by the Selling Pressure Index, which had been in an uptrend since early June, suggesting a pattern of increased selling into the rally. Selling Pressure continued to expand during the two-week October pullback by the DJIA with a sharp spike higher, indicating an increase in supply.

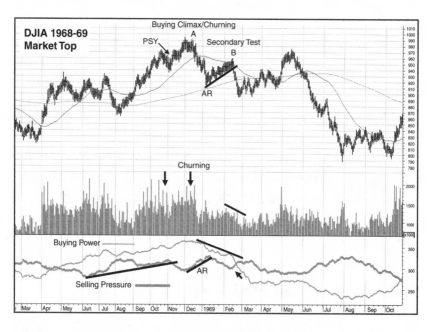

Charts created with Metastock, a Thomson Reuters product.

Figure 2.2   The initial phase of the 1968-69 major market top

However, demand was still apparent, as indicated by an uptrending Buying Power Index. As a result, the rally quickly resumed, carrying to the final high in November–December. Although a classic Wyckoff top calls for a Buying Climax at this point, the top in 1969 was a better representative of another Wyckoff principle, the Law of Effort vs. Result (in the form of a heavy volume churn). As is evident from the chart at point A, although volume remained heavy, the DJIA was unable to make any further progress after reaching a high on

November 29. A rally on heavy volume that fails to make any upside progress suggests aggressive selling into the advance. Coming on top of an extended rally and following the initial signs of increased selling offered by the PSY, such churning suggests a significant market top has been reached. But it is the subsequent movement in prices that confirms whether or not a major top is forming.

After about a week of churning and making no upside progress, Demand dried up, and prices began to fall into the Automatic Reaction (Point AR). Although volume was irregular on the Automatic Reaction pullback, the rise in Selling Pressure was a clear indication sellers were aggressively unloading stocks. However, prices were not yet ready to fall into a protracted decline, as the DJIA again rebounded to a recovery high at the Secondary Test at Point B. Volume on this rebound, however, was light and failed to expand, both aspects typical of an advance with limited upside potential. A continued slide in Buying Power offered additional evidence of a lack of demand behind the advance. The subsequent decline to the February low, however, occurred on decreasing volume and only a nominal rise in Selling Pressure. In fact, although the DJIA dropped below its January low in early February and again in mid-March, the corresponding peak in Selling Pressure was below its early January high. This lower peak in March suggested sellers were content to move to the sidelines, setting the stage for another attempt to rally the market. Rather than marking a renewed bull market, though, this rally began the final stage of the topping process, a process covered in the next chapter.

The Top of the 1970–1973 Bull Market

Starting in May 1970, the DJIA began a long bull run that eventually terminated at a high in early 1973. Figure 2.3 shows the last few months of this rally along with the indications a final top was in place.

The initial warning of a market top is at Point A, Preliminary Supply (PSY). Typically, PSY is marked by a surge in volume on a pullback, suggesting aggressive selling. In this case, though, while volume does show an increase, it is no higher than the volume accompanying the rally from the October reaction low. However, Lowry's Selling Pressure Index tells a different story. After showing a steady decline over the prior few months, Selling Pressure shows a sharp increase coincident with the December pullback in the DJIA (Point A). In fact, this increase in Selling Pressure comes close to breaking a multi-month downtrend.

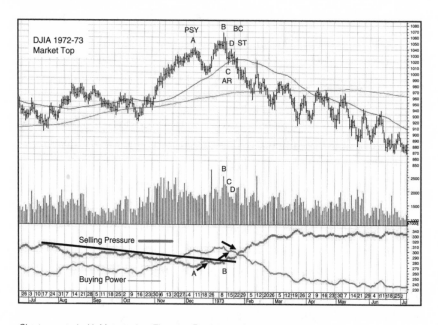

Charts created with Metastock, a Thomson Reuters product.

Figure 2.3   The initial phase of the 1972-73 market top

Rather than continuing lower, though, the DJIA resumes its rally in late December. Demand continues to increase, as indicated by the rise in Buying Power. But something else interesting is also happening. Although prices continue to climb into the Buying Climax, marked by the sharp rise in volume at Point B, Selling Pressure rises as well, with its low at the Buying Climax (Point B) well above its low at the bottom of the PSY reaction (Point A). This continued rise in Selling Pressure suggests supply continues to expand, even as prices are rising into the Buying Climax.

The drop into the Automatic Reaction (Point C) and rally back to the Secondary Test (Point D) had all the signs of a rally that has run out its string. Volume is heavy on the pullback to the low of the Automatic Reaction, suggesting active selling into the decline. An expansion in Supply was confirmed by another sharp rise in Selling Pressure, while the drop in Buying Power suggested little interest in buying the pullback. The subsequent rally to the high of the Secondary Test (Point D) occurred on a substantial decrease in volume from the rally to the Buying Climax high. The lack of Demand behind the rebound was also reflected by the minimal increase in Buying Power, while continued selling into the rally was evident in the nominal drop in Selling Pressure. Although the progression from PSY to the Secondary Test occurred over a relatively short period of time, the process appeared to portray a market where control has passed from buyers to sellers in preparation for the descent into a new bear market.

The Top of the 1975–1976 Bull Market

The end of the 1972–74 bear market was followed by a sharp rally beginning in December 1974 that carried the DJIA nearly 50% higher by mid-May 1975. The DJIA then traded generally sideways for about next seven months. But beginning in early December 1975, prices spiked sharply higher into the end of February 1976, doing so on very heavy volume. In Figure 2.4, the first suggestion all was not right with the rally was provided by the Selling Pressure Index. Despite a continued rise in prices, the Index began to rise in mid-January. This increase suggested that, rather than waiting for still higher prices, sellers were becoming more aggressive in dumping stock into the rally. Thus the warning flags were out when prices reacted lower on heavy volume in early February. The volume on this pullback suggested a possible point of Preliminary Supply (PSY at Point A) had been reached.

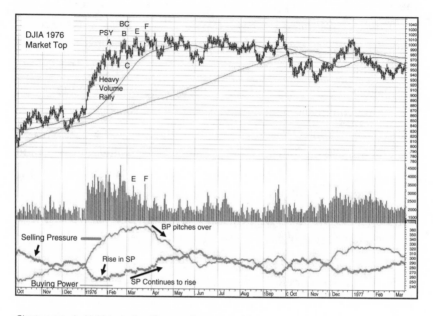

Charts created with Metastock, a Thomson Reuters product.

Figure 2.4   The initial phase of the 1976 major market top

The DJIA quickly recovered from the early February sell-off, though, surging higher on a spike in volume to a new rally high for the bull market in late February. However, this spike in volume at Point B suggested a potential Buying Climax (BC). Suspicions about a possible terminal move were supported by the Selling Pressure Index which had continued to rise during the DJIA's rally to the late February high. Prices quickly reacted lower after the Buying Climax in an Automatic Reaction. The decline to the Automatic Reaction low at Point C and subsequent rebound in the Secondary Test (Point E) provided further evidence of a rally in its final stages.

Volume remained heavy on the drop to the Automatic Reaction low, suggesting aggressive unloading of stock positions. Volume again spiked on rallies to the Secondary Test highs at Points E and F. However, despite the spikes in volume, prices failed to move substantially above the Buying Climax high. The failure to reach new highs suggested these rallies were being met with aggressive selling, symptomatic of distribution. Buying Power, however, continued a slow rise into the rally peak in late March. This rise suggested demand had not yet been totally exhausted, as late-comers to the bull market remained hopeful the market advance was still intact. At the same time, though, the steady rise in Selling Pressure suggested early buyers in the bull market were using the continued uptrend as an opportunity to unload more of their stock. The stalemate between rising demand and rising supply apparently ended in late March, when the Buying Power Index pitched over into a steep decline while Selling Pressure continued to rise. As things turned out, though, the bull had not yet breathed its last breath, and several months of further distribution were on tap before the DJIA tipped over into a bear decline.

The Top of the 1980–1981 Bull Market

The 1981 market top (Figure 2.5) marked the end of the cyclical bull markets in the 1966–82 secular bear market. From 1982 to 2000, bear markets proved short-lived, averaging only about three months in duration and retracing only a nominal portion of the preceding bull market, as the equity market entered a prolonged period of steadily rising prices in the new secular bull trend.

The 1980–81 bull market was a short-lived advance that began on March 27, 1980, the so-called Silver Thursday, when the Hunt Brothers' Silver Bubble burst. Prices moved steadily higher thereafter through early August 1980 at which point the rally stalled and fell into a sideways trading pattern. The DJIA finally broke out from this trading range in mid-November, reaching a new rally high a few days later. However, signs of a weakening bull market began to develop prior to that early August top. As of mid-July, Selling Pressure began a steady climb while Buying Power fell into a decline, suggesting a pattern of expanding supply and contracting demand. Although volume spiked higher in the rally to the November high, the DJIA was unable to hold its gain, dropping sharply into a reaction low in mid-December. This sharp decline suggested sellers were using the decline as an opportunity to dump stock positions. In addition, the drop to mid-December was accompanied by steady to rising volume, a sharp rise in Selling Pressure and the first appearance of a 90% Down Day in a market top since 1946. The heavy selling indicated by the 90% Down Day and rising volume provided a good indication of aggressive selling and that a point of Preliminary Supply (PSY, Point A) had been reached.

Charts created with Metastock, a Thomson Reuters product.

Figure 2.5   The initial phase of the 1980-81 major market top

Prices, however, were not yet ready to enter a bear trend as renewed demand was found just below the late October reaction low in the DJIA. The result was a rebound to a new rally high on January

6. Volume spiked higher on the rally to the January 6 high and then even higher on the decline on January 7 in a classic Buying Climax (BC Point B). Selling Pressure, however, showed only a small drop in the rally from mid-December to the Buying Climax high. At the same time, Buying Power showed only a nominal gain, suggesting demand was of low quality in the spike to the Buying Climax high. That is, the panic buying represented by the climactic price/volume resulted in stock positions immediately vulnerable to any reversal in the rally. In other words, this stock was now in weak hands.

As a result, rather than viewing the pullback following the Buying Climax as a buying opportunity, those weak hands began to aggressively unload stock as the decline was accompanied by another 90% Down Day. Panic selling again appeared as the decline to the Automatic Reaction low (AR, Point C) was completed with another 90% Down Day. A third 90% Down Day since the DJIA had reached its preliminary high in mid-November suggested sellers were clearly gaining control of the market. However, this control was not complete given that prices stabilized as the DJIA found support at its 200-day moving average. Enough demand emerged at this presumed support level to lift the DJIA back into another rally that carried to a first Secondary Test (ST) of the Buying Climax high in early March (Point D) and then to a second test later in the month (Point E). Volume rose steadily in the rally from the February test of the 200-day moving average, suggesting renewed demand.

That rally proved short-lived though. Despite heavy volume, the advance failed to move substantially above the level reached at the Buying Climax. Heavy volume that fails to produce corresponding price gains is evidence of churning, which itself is symptomatic of distribution. Clearly, supply was beginning to overcome demand. Churning was also evident in failure of the Buying Power Index to show any gain from its mid-March peak to the late April rally high in the DJIA. At the same time, Selling Pressure failed to show any significant loss. This suggested investors were using the rally to the late

March high as an opportunity to dump stocks rather than chase prices higher. As events played out, the March–April churning served as a warning the market was about to roll over into a new bear trend.

The Top of the 2003–2007 Bull Market

The market top inaugurating what many regard as the current secular bear trend formed in 2000–2001. Chapter 8, "The Curious Case of the 2000-2001 Market Top and Demise of the Secular Bull Market," is devoted to the many unique features of this major market top. The second market peak in the secular bear market occurred in 2007 following the four-year bull market that began in March 2003.

The first indication the bull market might be in trouble began with a sharp drop in the DJIA beginning in mid-July 2007 (Figure 2.6). After a brief recovery, the decline resumed, finally ending with a minor selling climax (Point A) in mid-August. The significant surge in volume accompanying the pullback suggested a point of Preliminary Supply (PSY) might have been reached. Two other factors suggested a significant change in the character of the rally. First, the decline from the July high to the August low was accompanied by four 90% Down Days, indicating intense selling. Except for the three that occurred in 1980–81, 90% Down Days were extremely rare at major market tops. One theory for the sudden proliferation of 90% Days in 2007 places responsibility on the elimination in July of the Up-Tick Rule for short selling. Whatever the merits of this theory, the presence of four 90% Down Days, plus the rise in volume, appeared to provide clear evidence a point of PSY had been reached in the July–August decline. The other factor suggesting a significant change in character for the market was the move by Lowry's Selling Pressure Index above Buying Power (Point B). This cross has, historically, been a signal supply is dominating demand.

Prices were not yet ready to fall into a bear trend, however, as the August selling climax met support at the DJIA 200-day moving average. Buying appeared intense at times during the subsequent rebound rally, given the three 90% Up Days accompanying the advance. However, overall volume failed to show any significant rise and remained well below the level on the drop from the July high to August reaction low. More importantly, the trend in demand failed to expand on the move to the October high, as Buying Power was flat to lower during the rally. At the same time, sellers remained active, as indicated by the nominal drop in the Selling Pressure Index.

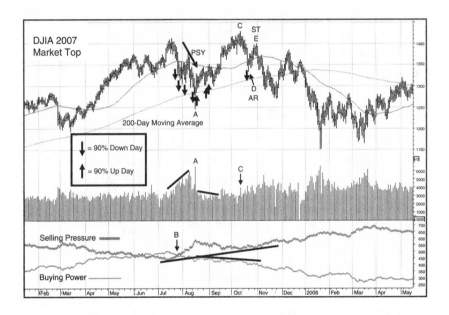

Charts created with Metastock, a Thomson Reuters product.

Figure 2.6   The initial phase of the 2007 major market top

What is conspicuous by its absence in this topping process is a Buying Climax. About the closest the DJIA could come to a Buying Climax was the failed rally on the spike to the ultimate high in the bull market on October 11, which was accompanied by a modest surge in volume (Point C). More significantly, though, was the fact Buying Power, at the October peak in the DJIA was well below its level at the July market high, despite the higher high in price. At the same time the low in Selling Pressure at the October market peak was far above its July low, suggesting much more aggressive unloading of stock. This aggressive selling was further evident during the subsequent drop to the Automatic Reaction low (AR, Point D) in late October, which occurred on a rise in volume, increase in Selling Pressure, and yet another 90% Down Day. Clearly, this pullback was not seen as a buying opportunity but as potentially a last chance for dumping stocks before a significant decline set in.

The rebound from the Automatic Reaction low to the Secondary Test (ST, Point E) managed to occur on a small rise in volume. However, Buying Power continued to fall, indicating the increase in volume was unlikely to represent the start of a trend of strengthening demand. Also the fact the rebound failed well below the October high in the DJIA, despite the rise in volume, suggested the rally was being met by significant new Supply. Again, this failed rally represents a potentially major change in character for the rally. Had expectations been for higher prices, then the rally should have induced new buying from those worried about missing the next leg higher in the bull market. Instead, the rally was met by enough selling to turn prices lower again, evidently the result of those worried about the possibility of having to sell at even lower prices.

In fact, those worries proved well-founded, as the rally to the Secondary Test in late October (Point E) proved to be the last gasp for the bull. What followed was the completion of the distribution process and descent into the bear market of 2007–2009, a process discussed in the following chapter.

3

How Major Market Tops Form:
Part II, The End Game

Major market tops generally form in two phases. The first phase, as discussed in the previous chapter, marks the end of an uptrend and the start of a process of distribution. During the first phase, however, buyers remain active, buoyed by hope the bull market is merely resting. This hope is reinforced by most economic data, which remains upbeat and pointing toward continued growth. Earnings for individual companies remain strong with analyst estimates indicating continued growth for the quarters ahead. But the stock market is a discounting mechanism, with prices based on expectations, not current conditions. Consequently, market tops are not made amid gloomy predictions of a slowing economy or recession, but when conditions for future growth may appear brightest. Likewise, major market bottoms occur when the outlook seems darkest—a primary reason why so many investors sell at or close to a bear market low and then are reluctant to re-enter when a new bull market begins.

In the second phase of a major top, signs of buyer fatigue become more evident, while selling becomes more aggressive. Typically, buyers become increasingly discouraged, as fewer and fewer stocks keep pace with gains in the market indexes. But with the proper tools, an alert investor can recognize this second and final phase of a major market top and prepare for the arrival of a new bear trend. As was the case with the initial phase of a major top, a combination of the Wyckoff and Lowry analyses can help an investor successfully recognize signs the topping process is concluding and a sustained market decline has begun.

Idealized Major Market Topping Pattern (Part II)

As described in the previous chapter, the first phase of a major market top marks the end of the bull market and start of the process of distributing stock from strong to weak hands. This phase begins with Preliminary Supply (PSY)—the first sign of major weakness in the market uptrend. This sign of weakness, as shown in Figure 3.1, is followed by a renewed rally, which typically ends with panic buying as investors, worried about missing the next big up move, pile into the market. This is the Buying Climax (BC). But buying at this point is of poor quality (that is, early buyers are selling to the latecomers to the bull market). Thus the climactic buying is short-lived as new Supply quickly swamps Demand. This rise in Supply results in a pullback termed the Automatic Reaction (AR).

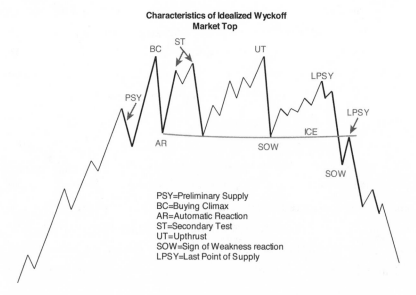

Figure 3.1   Wyckoff's key points for identifying a major market top

However, because there seems to be no evidence suggesting an imminent end to the bull market—that is, economic news and earnings are still good—late buyers see the pullback as an opportunity to scoop up stocks at lower prices. This buying produces a rebound rally termed the Secondary Test (ST). Depending on the length of the distribution process, there may be one or several Secondary Test rebound rallies before the market falls into a new bear trend. In this chapter, we examine the elements of the Wyckoff and Lowry analyses indicating the distribution process has ended and a new bear market begun. These elements are illustrated in Figure 3.1, beginning with the Upthrust after Distribution (UT).

Although not present in every major market top, the Upthrust (UT) or Upthrust after Distribution, is usually a clear indication the process of distribution is close to an end. The Upthrust may take prices to a new high or may test the highs formed during the earlier Secondary Tests. Typically the Upthrust occurs on moderate to heavy volume, as buyers hope to catch a new upleg in the bull market. However, the Upthrust typically proves short-lived, as prices quickly fall back. The Upthrust will also often signal the last gasp for strong Demand.

The pullback following the Upthrust generally occurs on moderate to heavy volume. This is because much of the stock bought on the Upthrust is in weak hands, that is, buyers who face almost immediate losses on any market pullback. A decline on light volume, though, will often lead to a rebound rally that serves as a test of the Upthrust. Light volume is key to this rebound rally, as a heavy volume rally would suggest enough renewed Demand to send prices to new highs, possibly voiding the topping process. While most Upthrusts are tested, there are some instances when they are not tested. In these cases, the investor should examine the price/volume action preceding the Upthrust. If volume tends to decrease on the rallies and increase on the reactions, representing distribution, the probabilities are that any move through the top of the trading range will be an Upthrust. Evidence of heavier volume on the rallies and lighter volume on the reactions that represent accumulation, however, would suggest the move to a new high is the start of a new upleg in the bull market.

There is also a variation of the Upthrust termed a Terminal Upthrust. In this case, the move above the trading range is more pronounced and occurs on heavy volume. Like an ordinary Upthrust, the Terminal Upthrust might or might not be tested. However, while ordinary Upthrusts can occur at any point during the formation of a major top, Terminal Upthrusts typically occur toward the end of the topping process. In reality, the Upthrust is considered a sign of weakness, largely for what it fails to do: result in a sustained breakout from the trading range.

A second indication the topping process is concluding is the Sign of Weakness (SOW) reaction. This SOW can follow an Upthrust or simply after a test of the top of the trading range. The key element to a SOW is the combination of a sharp decline in price and significant rise in volume. This combination indicates Supply is now moving into the dominant position. Unless this combination of heavy volume and sharp decline is obvious, though, the probabilities are the pullback is not a SOW, but simply a normal pullback within an ongoing trading range.

Despite the fact that selling is heavy on the SOW reaction, the pullback is often seen as another buying opportunity by those who remain focused on forecasts for continued economic gains and earnings growth. This very late-in-the-game buying produces a rebound rally resulting in a move to the Last Point of Supply (LPSY). This rebound rally will typically retrace half or less of the SOW sell-off and occur on light or diminishing volume. The low volume is key to the rebound, as a heavy volume rebound, especially one retracing more than half the SOW pullback, would suggest more strength than is usually associated with a rally to a LPSY. Such a rally would suggest the topping formation, rather than being near an end, still has further to run.

After a LPSY has been recorded, all that is left in the topping process is the final breakdown from the trading range. In Wyckoff parlance, this breakdown is termed Falling through the Ice. Unlike the straight line drawn across lows at about equal levels at the bottom of a trading range, the Ice is frequently a meandering, curved line, connecting lows at different levels as the formation of the trading range progressed. Its counterpart at a major market bottom is the Creek, which represents the key resistance level in a major bottoming pattern. Ideally, the Fall through the Ice should occur on heavy or expanding volume, suggesting a level of intense selling and expanding Supply associated with a sustainable decline. Usually, the Fall through the Ice is followed by a rebound rally to test the breakdown. This rebound should occur on significantly less volume than on the breakdown, as a light volume rebound would suggest the drop in prices has generated very little new buying interest. A rebound on heavy volume, however, would indicate strong Demand inconsistent with a sustainable breakdown. Such a heavy volume rally back above the Ice would suggest a more extensive rebound is in place. A rebound of this extent would, therefore, call for a reset of the sequence of signs of weakness leading to a breakdown. That is, new evidence of a SOW reaction, LPSY rebound, and subsequent Fall through the Ice.

A light volume rebound after a Fall through the Ice, however, would likely serve as a final LPSY. This LPSY below the level of the Ice constitutes the sell signal for the purpose of avoiding the bear market. And with a failure to break back through the Ice, the topping process is likely complete, with prices now poised to fall into a new bear market.

Using Lowry's Measures of Supply and Demand to Supplement the Wyckoff Analysis

As was the case with the initial signs of a market top—Preliminary Supply, Buying Climax, Automatic Reaction, Secondary Test—Lowry indicators can prove helpful in identifying those Wyckoff points occurring toward the end of a major topping pattern. Oftentimes, patterns can be less than clear cut in terms of showing rising or falling, light or heavy volume. In these cases, rising or falling Demand, as measured by the Buying Power Index and changes in Supply, as indicated by the Selling Pressure Index, can help clarify conflicting or indefinite volume patterns.

For instance, the key to identifying a Sign of Weakness (SOW) reaction is heavy volume. Yet volume itself may be inconsistent during the pullback, varying between heavy, moderate or even light on a day to day basis. In this case, steadily rising Selling Pressure and falling Buying Power would suggest the increasing Supply associated with a valid SOW reaction. Similarly, a rally to a Last Point of Supply (LPSY) accompanied by increased Selling Pressure and decreased Buying Power would be a good indication of a lack of Demand behind the advance and of continued active selling into the rally.

Let's turn now to see how all these Wyckoff and Lowry indications work out in real life by examining the final stages of the market tops discussed in Chapter 2, "How Major Market Tops Form: Part I, The Preliminaries."

Final Stages of the 1968–1969 Market Top

We left the 1968–69 market top as prices had topped at the mid February Secondary Test and were dropping to the late February reaction low. Volume steadily contracted on this decline, while Selling Pressure showed only a nominal rise—both indications prices were

not yet ready to tip over into a new bear market. However, things
were about to change.

Charts created with Metastock, a Thomson Reuters product.

Figure 3.2   The final phase of the 1968-69 major market top

As shown in Figure 3.2, from the February low, the DJIA began
an irregular advance to mid-April (Point A). Volume failed to show
any significant rise during this rally and, with the exception of a couple brief spikes higher, was generally less than on the decline to the
February low. Clearly, the lower prices reached in late February
failed to attract any significant buying interest. The lack of Demand
behind the rally was also reflected in the Buying Power Index, which
initially continued to fall into mid March and then turned flat through
the April 1969 rally high. At the same time, Selling Pressure
increased into mid March and then turned lower. The lack of expanding Demand, though, was probably the best warning the rally did not
represent the start of a major move higher. However, the next

rebound in prices, in late April, which began from a level well above the February and March lows, appeared to reignite buying interest, as the DJIA quickly spiked higher, accompanied by a huge increase in volume on April 30 (Point B). The quick spike higher on very heavy volume is characteristic of an Upthrust, even if it did not carry above the November rally highs. The characterization of this spike higher as an Upthrust is reinforced by the subsequent struggle to extend the rally.

While the DJIA gained 25 points (925–950) in just two sessions—April 29–30, 1969—the Average spent the next ten sessions rising just 18 points (950–968). As volume remained heavy over this period, it is evident sellers were using the advance to unload their remaining positions. This was likely particularly true of those who had bought around the market top in early November and were then trapped by the subsequent quick decline. Also note that, despite the rally to this mid-May high, there was very little expansion in Buying Power and only a modest contraction in Selling Pressure, further evidence of exhausted Demand but continued active selling. The struggle to follow through on the late April spike in prices, lack of Demand and active Selling all helped define the May high as a Last Point of Supply (LPSY Point C).

Volume was moderate to light during the first two weeks of decline from the mid May LPSY but began to show a significant rise by early June. This rise in volume was reinforced by a simultaneous jump in Selling Pressure. The increase in both volume and Selling Pressure indicated the decline was, in fact, a Sign of Weakness (SOW). In this case, the rise in Supply coincided with a Fall through the Ice (Point D), marked by the line connecting the December, February, March, and April lows. This early-June breakdown through the Ice was subsequently followed by a test in early July (Point E). Buying was half-hearted, though, as indicated by the very light volume on the rally and the further drop in Buying Power. At the same time, there was a minimal drop in Selling Pressure, which was now in a clear-cut uptrend. All this suggested the rally in early July constituted a Last Point of Supply below the Ice and, as such, the sell signal for investors. And, in fact, this modest rally proved to be the last gasp for the bulls, as the DJIA fell from here into a bear market that lasted until late May, 1970, and took the Average to a low at 631, for a loss of 354 points (36%).

The End of the 1972–1973 Market Top

Unlike the top of the 1966–69 bull market, things unraveled quickly after the Secondary Test (Point D) at the top of the 1970–73 bull market (Figure 3.3). As noted in the previous chapter, the rally to the Secondary Test was accompanied by a substantial decrease in volume, only a nominal increase in Buying Power and slight increase in Selling Pressure. However, no period of distribution followed the Secondary Test, as the DJIA quickly fell into a SOW reaction. Although volume was irregular on the decline (Point E), the sharp rise in Selling Pressure offered graphic evidence of the heavy and increasing selling into the decline. Further evidence of rising Supply was provided by the move in Selling Pressure to the dominant position above Buying Power, suggesting sellers were then in control. This move in Selling Pressure to the dominant position also constitutes a sell signal according to the Lowry analysis. At the same time, buyers showed little stomach for bargain hunting, as the Buying Power Index went into a steep decline, demonstrating a sharp contraction in Demand. In this case, the SOW reaction also encompassed a Break through the Ice (Point F) in late January.

The decline following the break below the Ice was temporarily interrupted by an attempted rebound after a test of the DJIA 200-day moving average (Point G). This rebound apparently motivated some bargain hunting and possibly some premature short-covering, as prices quickly spiked higher. The rally ended just as quickly, though, with a very heavy volume attempt to break back through the Ice on February 13, 1973 (Point H). This heavy volume spike evidently served to exhaust whatever Demand still existed, as prices immediately turned lower, helping identify the spike as a likely LPSY and the sell signal for investors. The status of the February 13 spike as a LPSY was then confirmed by the pickup in volume and rapid rise in Selling Pressure as the DJIA fell below the early February reaction low.

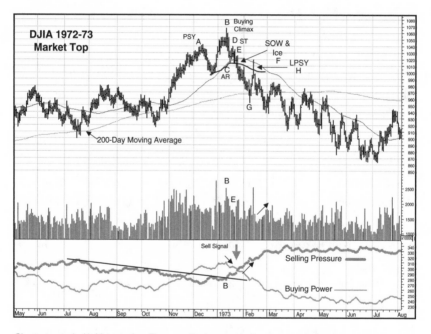

Charts created with Metastock, a Thomson Reuters product.

Figure 3.3   The final phase of the 1972-73 major market top

This relatively brief, seven-week topping pattern suggests a long period of distribution is not necessarily needed prior to a major market decline, considering the 1972–74 bear market was the worst modern day bear after the 1929–32 bear market—that is, until it was surpassed by the 2007–2009 market debacle.

The Drawn-Out Conclusion to the 1976 Market Top

In contrast to the relatively compact major top at the end of the 1970–72 bull market, the demise of the 1975–76 bull market was a more drawn-out affair through much of 1976 (Figure 3.4). The initial phase of the market top played out over a relatively brief time span, with Preliminary Supply (PSY), the Buying Climax (BC), Automatic Reaction (AR) and Secondary Test (ST) all occurring within a six-week span. This initial phase of the top ended in late March 1976, as Buying Power fell into a steep decline and Selling Pressure continued to climb.

Charts created with Metastock, a Thomson Reuters product.

Figure 3.4   The final phase of the 1976 major market top

Volume remained relatively light on the pullback from the mid-April 1976 high (Point A), suggesting sellers were at least temporarily stepping to the sidelines. The modest rise in Selling Pressure on the drop to the early May low also suggested a reduced Supply of stock for sale. If sellers were waiting for higher prices, their patience was rewarded with a rebound from the early May low, as the DJIA tested its mid April high on heavy volume (Point B).

This rally's failure to push to a new high, despite the spike in volume, suggested the continued presence of heavy Supply at the level of the April high. Sellers marked this failure as another opportunity to unload stocks, resulting in the drop to the early June low (Point C). Although Selling Pressure continued to rise, there was no significant increase in volume, suggesting the decline was not the SOW that typically accompanies the end phase of the topping process. And in fact, prices stabilized just below the February-April lows, as buyers at those prior lows once again stepped back into the market. Volume showed a steady increase on the rally from the June 1976 low. The increase in Demand and decrease in Supply on the rally was further supported by a new rise in Buying Power and drop in Selling Pressure. All this provided evidence the topping process still had further to run.

Any hope that this period of churning, from February through May 1976, had been just an interruption in a continuing bull market were dashed, though, when the advance ran out of steam back at the rally highs from March, April and May (Point D). This failure to push to new rally highs, despite what was now a pattern of expanding Demand and contracting Supply (rising Buying Power, falling Selling Pressure), was another piece of evidence the bull market was in serious jeopardy. Sellers, though, seemed content to sit on their stock, as the July high was followed by two months of sideways churning and falling Selling Pressure. This churning ended with a renewed decline that tested support at the June low and the DJIA's 200-day moving average (Point E). The rebound from the 200-day moving average suggests that once again sellers had failed to send the DJIA to a new reaction low. This failure evidently resurrected hopes by the late-to-the-party crowd of another leg up in the bull market and an opportunity for the profits they had missed during the 1975 market rally. The result was the sharp rally on expanding volume to a marginal new high in mid-September 1976 (Point F).

An examination of trading over the prior seven months, however, should have created second thoughts for those buyers who ventured into the rally up to the September high. If the seven-month sideways pattern were leading to a new up leg in the bull market, measures of Supply and Demand should have indicated a process of accumulation. Instead, at the September market peak, Buying Power was far below its level in late March and Selling Pressure was clearly above its January-February lows. So instead of showing a pattern of expanding Demand and contracting Supply consistent with accumulation, Buying Power and Selling Pressure indicated a process of distribution—that is, rising Supply and falling Demand.

Thus, an alert investor would have suspected that the spike by the DJIA to a new high on very heavy volume on September 22 (Point F), was more likely a buying climax than the start of a new up leg in the bull market. And in fact, the climactic action represented the final exhaustion in Demand in a clear illustration of a Wyckoff-defined Terminal Upthrust.

From this point, the final topping process unfolded quickly. Although volume failed to show a significant increase on the decline from the September high, Selling Pressure told a different story, as the Index showed the sharpest rise of the whole topping process. The SOW reaction also served as a breakdown through the Ice (at Point G), formed by a line connecting the June and August reaction lows in the DJIA. The significance of the Break through the Ice was emphasized by a move in Selling Pressure above Buying Power, registering a Lowry sell signal. The SOW also carried to a new reaction low, suggesting that whatever Demand had existed at the June and August lows, was now gone. While prices finally stabilized at a lower level, the resulting rally was on light volume and contracting Buying Power. This suggested the rebound was probably more the result of short-covering than longer-term buying, typical of a rally to the Last Point of Supply. This LPSY, in turn, served as the sell signal for investors.

There was one last gasp for the bull market though, as the DJIA, after recording a slightly lower low in early November, began to rally. This rally could probably be best described as a secondary topping pattern. Without question, the rally began strongly enough to call into question whether the whole process over the past nine months did, in fact, represent a topping pattern. Volume in the early stages of the rally from the November low was heavy, while there was a sharp rise in Buying Power and equal drop in Selling Pressure. Certainly, the bull market appeared to be once again firing on all cylinders. However, as the DJIA approached the levels of the rally highs from March, April, May, and July 1976, volume began to fade, and Supply began to expand, as indicated by the rise in Selling Pressure (Point H). As the DJIA tipped over into a renewed decline in early January 1977, volume remained heavy, suggesting sellers were once again aggressively unloading their stock—action inconsistent with only a temporary setback for the market. And, in fact, the late December high represented the final recovery peak after which the DJIA descended into a bear market that would last until 1980.

The Less Drawn-Out 1980–1981 Market Top

At about eight months from start to finish, the top of the 1980–81 bull market (Figure 3.5) was not as compact as the three-month top in 1973 but not as lengthy as the thirteen-month top in 1976. Nonetheless, the top in 1980–81 marked a watershed for the stock market, as it proved to be the final top in the 16 year secular bear market that began in 1966.

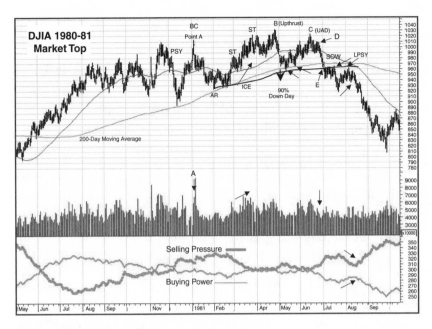

Charts created with Metastock, a Thomson Reuters product.

Figure 3.5　The final phase of the 1980-81 major market top

The preceding chapter left the initial phase of the 1980–81 top at the late March 1981 Secondary Test (ST) of the January Buying Climax (Point A). The late March assault on the level reached at the Buying Climax occurred on rising volume, suggesting buyers were, as yet, unconvinced the bull market from the 1980 market bottom was finished. However, this enthusiasm evidently had its limits, as the rally faltered just above the level of the January high. After a brief bout of profit-taking, a second assault and Secondary Test was mounted in early April. But this move came on much lighter volume, suggesting much of the remaining Demand for stocks had been exhausted in the rally a week or so earlier. Most telling, however, was the failure of Buying Power to expand or Selling Pressure to contract on the rally to the April high. This suggested the move to the March high had significantly diminished available Demand while there was little reduction in selling.

There was one last effort to rejuvenate the bull market, as a renewed burst of buying managed to lift the DJIA to a new recovery high in late April (Point B). Although volume was relatively heavy on the rally, the gains were short-lived as prices immediately fell into a sharp decline. This quick reversal of the move to a new rally high is a classic example of an Upthrust. Prices dropped sharply over the next week, but on relatively light volume, suggesting a test of the Upthrust was likely to occur. As had occurred on the declines from Preliminary Supply and at the lows on the Automatic Reaction, prices found support at the rising 200-day moving average for the DJIA. And a 90% Down Day on May 4 suggested Supply may have been at least temporarily exhausted, given that day's heavy selling.

However, having been burned in the rally to the Upthrust in April (Point B) and subsequent quick reversal, buyers were evidently reluctant to aggressively pursue stocks, as the rally from the 200-day moving average began on light volume. After a brief bounce, a pullback in late May also found support at the 200-day moving average. This second test of support evidently emboldened buyers who concluded a significant new move higher had begun, as volume showed a sharp rise. Instead, the rally proved to be nothing more than the anticipated test of the Upthrust, as the rally peaked in mid-June (Point C), just below the high set in late April. This test could also be considered a final Upthrust, or Upthrust After Distribution (UAD). After a brief pullback, buyers mounted a weak effort to recoup the losses (Point D). However, volume on the effort was very light, and the rebound failed after retracing about half the decline from the June high—clear indications that whatever enthusiasm there had been for a renewed rally was now gone.

This weak rebound effort was evidently the signal sellers had been waiting for, as prices plunged over the next few sessions, quickly slicing through what had been key support at the DJIA 200-day moving average. Something clearly had changed, as the buying support previously found at the moving average had disappeared. The seriousness of this late June/early July decline was highlighted by the action of the Buying Power and Selling Pressure Indexes. Both had remained relatively flat on the rally to the mid-June test of the Upthrust, but now Selling Pressure spiked higher while Buying Power showed a sharp decline. The combination of the sharp drop in prices and jump in Supply suggested the decline represented a Sign of Weakness (SOW) reaction. The drop below support at the 200-day moving average also resulted in a Break below the Ice (Point E), signaling the approaching end of the topping process.

Prices lingered just below the 200-day moving average in the process forming a LPSY and a clear sell signal for investors. Volume remained light on a series of attempts to break back up through the Ice, indicating that, despite the violation of key support, prices had not dropped low enough to generate any strong buying interest. However, the bull market was not quite ready to expire. The early July sideways trading was apparently concluded by the sharp decline in mid-July 1981. But the decline proved short-lived, however, as buyers re-emerged at about the level of the January Automatic Reaction low. After all, that low had resulted in a nearly three-month rally that carried prices to new highs. Maybe a repeat performance was on tap.

The rally over the next couple of weeks, though, appeared primarily due to short-covering (premature covering, as it turned out) and some desultory bargain hunting. Most significantly, volume remained light on the rebound, while gains in Buying Power were substantially less than the losses in Selling Pressure. This pattern suggested the rally was due more to a withdrawal of Supply than strong Demand— a combination typical of a Last Point of Supply. The final element of the topping process fell into place when the late July/early August rebound rally failed to move above the highs set by the early July sideways trading, thereby constituting a failure to break back up through the Ice and confirming its role as a Last Point of Supply, which, in this case constituted a terminal event and a second sell signal for any investors who failed to heed the first in mid-July. A weak effort to hold the July lows was short-lived and followed by a swift decline. This decline was accompanied by a sharp rise in Selling Pressure and drop in Buying Power, suggesting there would be no late-day rescue attempt, as occurred in the November/December rally of 1976. Instead, the DJIA continued to plunge in what was now a full-fledged bear market that would persist to the August 1982 low.

It is also worth noting that Supply moved to the dominant position above Demand early in the topping process when the Selling Pressure Index crossed above the Buying Power Index in early December 1980. Over the course of the rest of the next few months, as the market traded sideways, and despite several moves to new rally highs, Buying Power was never able to move back to a dominant position, further reinforcing the appearance of a market in the process of forming a major top rather than preparing for a significant move higher.

The Preamble to the Worst Bear Market Since 1929–1932—the Final Stages of the 2007 Market Top

The initial phase of the 2007 market top was completed with the rally to the Secondary Test (Point A, Figure 3.6) in late October. Despite the heavy volume on this rally, it failed well below the level of the early October market high, suggesting the advance was being met by increased selling. From this point, signs of weakness continued to grow until the final breakdown in early 2008.

When the rally to the ST high failed, selling began to snowball rather than shrink, and volume continued to expand on the pullback, indicating sellers were now rushing to exit the market. The intensity of selling was reinforced by two 90% Down Days. Further evidence of new weakness was the drop by the DJIA below its 200-day moving average, a level that had provided support in the drop to the mid-August and early September lows.

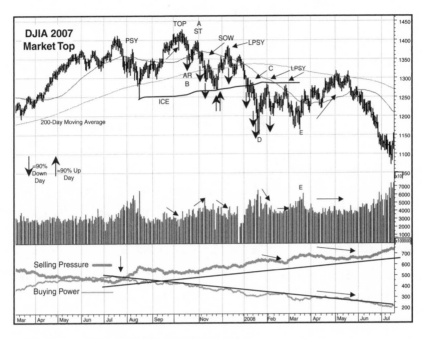

Charts created with Metastock, a Thomson Reuters product.

Figure 3.6   The final phase of the 2007 major market top

This drop below the 200-day moving average was confirmed by the failure of a weak and very brief rebound rally to make a sustained break back above the moving average. Heavy volume and intense selling are characteristics of a SOW decline—itself an indication the topping process was entering its terminal stage. However, the bull was not quite ready to expire, as the subsequent drop close to the August reaction low evidently inspired new hope among buyers the worst was over. This optimistic outlook was indicated by two 90% Up Days occurring at and just after the mid-November 2007 low. These indications of strong Demand clearly suggested the market was not yet ready to fall into a bear trend.

With sellers temporarily stepping to the sidelines, prices began another ascent, buoyed by the apparently successful test of the August low and the two 90% Up Days. However, an observant investor would likely notice volume failed to show any significant

expansion on this rally. The failure of volume to expand suggests buying of very poor quality, comprised largely of short-covering and
short-term bargain hunting. The clearest indication the rally produced no meaningful changes in the overall pattern of contracting
Demand and expanding Supply was provided by the Buying Power
and Selling Pressure Indexes. Rather than accompanying the rally
with a sharp rise, Buying Power managed only a marginal gain that
did nothing to change the downtrend in force since mid-July 2007. At
the same time, Selling Pressure was essentially flat, indicating selling
remained steady. Weak Demand, light volume, and steady selling
were all signs of an advance to a Last Point of Supply. The failure of
the rally to move above the level of the late October Secondary Test
only served to confirm its nature as a LPSY. The market was now on
the hinge for a final plunge into a full-fledged bear trend. However,
because this LPSY was still above the level of a breakdown (through
the Ice), it did not yet constitute a clear sell signal.

Indications that prices were headed lower came rapidly after the
LPSY peak, with a quick 90% Down Day, suggesting sellers were now
rushing for the exit. A weak rebound then failed to retrace no more
than half the initial decline from the LPSY, despite continued heavy
volume, suggesting the buying was again being met by heavy selling.
The failure of this rebound rally resulted in a steeper decline that
quickly took the DJIA below the lows set in mid-August and late
November 2007. This drop to a new reaction low provided clear evidence that, whatever Demand had existed at those prior lows, it was
now gone. And that's a formula for even lower prices.

In terms of the Wyckoff topping pattern, this decline represented
a Fall Below the Ice (Point C), a breakdown emphasized by yet
another 90% Day. Another weak rebound effort quickly failed, representing an unsuccessful attempt to move back above the Ice. This
failure then precipitated an avalanche of selling, as volume spiked
sharply higher and selling intensified with two more 90% Down
Days. This selling quickly reached climactic proportions, as evident

by the big move lower on January 18 followed by a sharp rebound on January 23, 2008, characteristic of a selling climax (Point D).

If a selling climax represents a major bottom, it should be followed by strong buying interest, as buyers enthusiastically snap up bargain-priced stocks. In this case, though, volume on the rally following the selling climax decreased from its level on the decline. Most telling was the very small drop in Selling Pressure. Another characteristic of an important selling climax is that it serves to exhaust Supply. Given the failure of Selling Pressure to show a sharp contraction on the rebound rally, it is clear Supply remained abundant as sellers once again used the rally as an opportunity to unload additional shares on unwitting buyers. The weakness of this rebound rally then became apparent as it failed around the same level as the short-lived early January test of the Ice. This latest rally, then, proved to be another failed test of the Ice, a failure that rapidly became evident to the sellers as it was followed immediately by another 90% Down Day. As such, this failed test could be considered a second Last Point of Supply. This second failure to break through the Ice, was the veritable horn-blowing, flag waving sign the top was in and prices were now headed into a major bear decline. This second LPSY was also a clear signal for investors to exit the market.

There were, though, another couple of opportunities to get out for those investors still clinging to the hope of a continuing bull market. The first occurred in the late February 2008 rally. While volume on the rally was generally light, the most telling evidence this was a short-lived rebound rally was provided by the Selling Pressure and Buying Power Indexes. Although prices rallied, Buying Power remained flat while Selling Pressure dropped, indicating gains were based more on a lack of Supply than expanding Demand. Thus, it was probably no surprise the rally failed at the same levels as the early December and late January rebounds. Clearly, the Supply that stopped those rallies was still there.

The decline following this third effort to break back above the Ice ended in a minor selling climax in mid-March (Point E). The subsequent rally finally managed to rise to new recovery highs, above those December, January and February peaks. Maybe things weren't so bad after all! However, there were two problems with the rally an observant investor might have noticed. First, once again, volume failed to rise on the rally, suggesting buyers were reluctant to follow prices higher. Second, Selling Pressure showed only a modest decline and maintained its longer term uptrend, suggesting sellers remained active in the rally. Third, and most telling, Buying Power also declined, suggesting a distinct lack of Demand behind the gains. This was a repeat of the same pattern of the rally to the late February recovery high, that is, an advance based more on contracting Supply than expanding Demand. That February rally ended badly, and so did this one, as the DJIA proceeded to lose 2000 points over the next couple months.

Each of the market tops described in these chapters is different, but each share common characteristics. Our purpose in presenting the histories of these market tops is to provide a guide to the key features of a major market topping formation so an investor may recognize them as they develop at future market peaks. And while the Wyckoff analysis provides a guide to identifying the key phases and turning points of a major top, the Lowry analysis helps to quantify the shift from dominant buyers to dominant sellers. With these tools, an investor should be well prepared to recognize major market tops as they develop and to take the necessary defensive moves to avoid the potentially catastrophic portfolio losses than can occur in a full-fledged bear market.

4

How Major Market Bottoms Form:
Part I, Panic and Capitulation

Chapters 2 and 3 focused on the life cycle of a major market uptrend and the subsequent formation of a major market top. Major market tops are characterized by distribution, that is, well informed investors liquidating shares of stocks in anticipation of lower prices in the coming months. Distribution is then followed by the markdown phase, which is the bulk of the bear market itself, or the process of stock prices trending lower. The markdown process can vary greatly in length. For example, the decline from the 1929 high lasted three long years, while the bear market of 1998 was a mere three months. As the markdown phase nears its end, signs of the final phase of the bear market—the all-important panic stage—emerge. Identifying the panic phase is critical, as it is quickly followed by the accumulation stage of the bear market bottom, during which investors begin the process of snapping up what they now perceive to be bargain-priced stocks. Recognizing the accumulation phase is particularly important because it is during this time when stocks should be purchased so that investors may reap the benefits of the developing bull market.

The Life Cycle of a Market Downtrend (a.k.a., A Bear Market)

By the end of a bull market and start of a new bear market, Demand has been exhausted, and Supply is the dominant force driving price action. As anyone who has taken a basic course in macroeconomics knows, when Supply is greater than Demand, prices fall. In the case of the stock market, the dominance of Supply results in a prolonged period of price deterioration. The psychological aspects of a stock market decline are described in Paul Desmond's Dow Award winning paper "Identifying Bear Market Bottoms and New Bull Markets":

> Important market declines are, for the most part, a study in the extremes of human emotion. The intensity of their emotions can be statistically measured through their purchases and sales. To clarify, as prices initially begin to weaken, investor psychology slowly shifts from complacency to concern, resulting in increased selling and an acceleration of the decline. As prices drop more quickly, and the news becomes more negative, the psychology shifts from concern to fear. Sooner or later, the fear turns to panic, driving prices sharply lower, as investors strive to get out of the market any price. It is this panic stage that drives prices down to extreme discounts—often well below book values—that is needed to set the stage for the next bull market.[1]

Just as bull market tops tend to follow similar patterns of distribution, major market bottoms tend to follow similar patterns of accumulation, reflecting the process of Demand overcoming Supply. While Richard Wyckoff identified these various stages of the idealized market bottom, L.M. Lowry's methods of identifying changes in the longer term trends of Supply and Demand provide a means for quantifying the stages identified by Wyckoff.

This chapter discusses the capitulation or panic phase of the bear market and the initial stage of accumulation, and Chapter 5, "How Major Market Bottoms Form: Part II, Accumulation and Breakout," details the characteristics of the final stages of accumulation and the evolution of a new bull market. In the course of our discussion, we draw from both Paul Desmond's white paper and Wyckoff's Stock Market Correspondence Course, as offered by the Stock Market Institute. Wyckoff's descriptive terms for the final phases of a bear market and early signs of accumulation are shown in Figure 4.1.

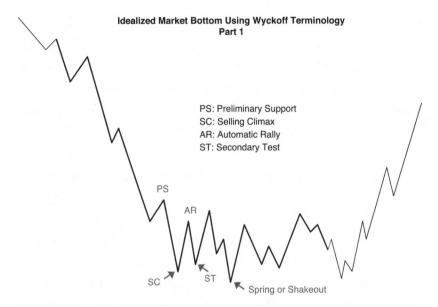

Figure 4.1   **Wyckoff's key points for identifying a major market bottom**

The first point of reference in the formation of a major market bottom is referred to as *Preliminary Support* (PS). Prior to the development of PS, negative momentum has tended to feed upon itself as the downtrend progresses. During this progression, the rate of decline can remain steady or accelerate as time goes on. The same may be said for volume during the decline, as it often remains steady or gradually increases as the downtrend progresses. Whichever the case, the bear market has plenty of fuel to keep it moving. Extremely heavy or light volume both work against the continuation of the decline by starving it in the case of light volume, or killing it in the case of very high volume. In the absence of either of these volume extremes, a rally of any consequence is hard to get. At some point, however, either through a sudden surge in volume or a lack of it to further fuel the decline, a notable rally will occur.[2]

This rally, termed Preliminary Support, should be notable in that it will stand out among other upside reactions during the bear market in terms of price gain and volume. While this advance may not travel far enough to break any important trend lines that defined the downtrend, it will often produce some type of break above an area of overhead Supply. The development of PS is especially likely as the market approaches the downside objective established by the point and figure count taken from the preceding major market top.[3]

At this point in the discussion, it is appropriate to introduce a component of the Lowry Analysis that is helpful in identifying PS as well as other stages of the formation of a major market bottoms: 90% Upside and 90% Downside Days. Paul Desmond, Lowry Research Corporation's President, introduced 90% Days at a meeting of the Market Technicians Association in 1982. The topic of 90% Days is elaborated upon extensively in Mr. Desmond's white paper, "Identifying Bear Market Bottoms and New Bull Markets."

The components that make up 90% Days are among the metrics Lowry Research compiles at the end of each trading day on the NYSE in order to create the Buying Power and Selling Pressure Indexes:

- Total point gains for stocks closing higher on the day
- Total volume for all stocks closing higher on the day
- Total point losses for all stocks closing lower on the day
- Total volume for all stocks closing lower on the day

A 90% Down Day occurs when Downside Volume equals 90% or more of total Upside Volume plus Downside Volume, *and* Points Lost equals 90% or more of the total of Points Gained plus Points Lost. 90% Downside Days are indicative of panic selling. Table 4.1 shows an example.

TABLE 4.1 NYSE Closing Points and Volume

Date	Upside Volume	Downside Volume	Points Gained	Points Lost	Upside Vol %	Upside Points %
11-12-10	435,489,094	3,829,991,034	80	1129	10.21%°	6.62%
11-15-10	1,838,873,888	1,754,066,919	336	342	51.18%	49.56%
11-16-10	313,920,635	5,020,625,050	53	1478	5.88%	3.46%

*Note that November 12 did not qualify as a 90% Downside Day. Although Points Lost breached the 90% threshold, Down Volume fell short, at 89.79% of Upside plus Downside Volume.

On November 16, Downside Volume equaled 94.12% of the sum of Upside plus Downside Volume:

5,020,625,050 / (313,920,635 + 5,020,625,050) x 100 = 94.12%

and, Points Lost equaled 96.54% of the sum of Points Gained plus Points Lost:

1478 / (53 + 1478) x 100 = 96.54%

A 90% Upside Day is the opposite of a 90% Downside Day, in that Upside Volume equals 90% or more of total Upside Volume plus Downside Volume, *and* Points Gained equals 90% or more of the total of Points Gained plus Points Lost.

Lowry's research into the development of major market bottoms found that, more often that not, in addition to occurring on a sharp rise in volume, Preliminary Support will also occur in the form of a 90% Upside Day. The development of this phenomenon allows for easier identification of a change in character for the market that had previously been in the midst of a persistent and major move lower.

The development of PS is not a call for action on the part of the investor, despite what appears to be a sudden burst of investor buying interest. Rather, it is more of a warning that the bear market may be nearing an end. Evidence that a valid point of PS has indeed been established occurs with the next step in the bottoming process: the Selling Climax (SC).

The Selling Climax occurs when investors realize the rally representing Preliminary Support was not the start of a major move higher. Instead, the market sells off to new bear market lows and as a result,

> ...a large number of shareholders who have resisted the urge to sell during the decline to that point come to the realization, at approximately the same time, of just how bad things are. This is followed by fear over just how much worse they may get, and this leads to wholesale dumping of stocks to avoid the expectation of what lies ahead. What actually happens is that the sudden and sustained increase in Supply precipitates the worst. The Selling Climax is accomplished when the Supply of shares to be sold is exhausted. At this point, the downward push is eliminated, and a rally develops.[4]

While the SC is the action that actually stops the decline, it may, at times, not represent the actual nadir of the bear market.

The mindset of investors at the SC stage of the bear market, characterized by fear and panic, drives holders of stocks to get out of the market at any price. "It is this panic that drives prices down to extreme discounts—often well below book values—that is needed to set the stage for the next bull market."[5] As a result, having a quantifiable method for identifying panic selling is critical in identifying the early stages of a major market bottom. This is where 90% Downside Days come into play, as subsequent examples of major market bottoms soon illustrate.

However, 90% Downside Days are not limited to the SC phase of a major bottoming formation. In fact, "historical record shows that 90% Down Days do not usually occur as a single incident on the bottom day of an important market decline, but typically occur on a number of occasions throughout a major decline, often spread apart by as much as thirty trading days."[6]

However, the final dumping of shares, or the SC, is often characterized by the development of more than one 90% Down Days in close proximity as the ultimate watershed selling takes place. In addition to the development of one or more 90% Down Days, heavy volume and wide daily price ranges also often occur during the SC.

While exhausted selling represents an important component in the formation of a major market low, a sustainable bottom cannot develop without evidence of enthusiastic investor Demand. This is where the next phase of the bottoming process, the Automatic Rally (AR), comes in. With Supply at least temporarily exhausted, a wave of buying enters in the market. This strong buying is often supplemented by added upside pressure from short covering, as those positioned for a further decline scramble to buy back shorted stocks when evidence of a meaningful rebound rally emerges. The AR often occurs in the form of one or more 90% Upside Days. Although the bottoming process is not yet complete, the combination of one or more 90% Downside Days followed by one or more 90% Upside Days (or, on rare occasions, two back-to-back 80% Upside Days) provides compelling evidence that a major trend reversal has begun.

The development of an AR in the form of a 90% Upside Day is important. As Paul Desmond states in his white paper,

> ...days of panic selling, by themselves, cannot produce a market reversal any more than simply lowering the sale price on a house will produce an enthusiastic buyer. As the Law of Supply and Demand would emphasize, it takes strong Demand, not just a reduction in Supply, to cause prices to rise substantially. It does not matter how much prices are discounted; if investors are not attracted to buy, even at deeply depressed levels, sellers will eventually be forced to discount prices further still, until Demand is eventually rejuvenated. Lowry's extensive history shows that declines containing two or more 90% Down Days usually persist, on a trend basis, until investors eventually come rushing back in to snap up what they perceive to be the bargains of the decade and, in the process, produce a 90% Upside Day.[7]

The Automatic Rally typically lasts for roughly a week. Its duration tends to be limited as it is built on a still rather shaky foundation, despite the potent combination of 90% Down Days and 90% Upside Days. As the Automatic Reaction progresses, those investors still looking to unload shares will use the rally to sell, not wanting to get caught up again in a painful downward spiral of prices. This renewed Supply will result in another wave of downward pressure on the market. As stated in the Wyckoff Course, "In addition, those who had the courage to buy at or near the climax know that there is no firm reason as yet to expect an important up move, so they tend to be content with a relatively small, quick gain."[8] The selling by those looking to sell old long positions and to take quick profits from well-timed purchases made during the Selling Climax work to stifle the life of the AR. Typically, the high of the AR represents the upper boundary of the trading range that represents the major market bottom.

The demise of the Automatic Rally is an important part of the bottoming process, as it leads into the next critical stage of the formation of a major market bottom, the Secondary Test (ST). As stated in the Wyckoff Course,

> No matter how classic the pattern appears to be as the low (of the Selling Climax) is hit and followed by an Automatic Rally, the Selling Climax becomes a reality only after it is confirmed. This is accomplished by the Secondary Test, which immediately follows the Automatic Rally. In order to successfully confirm the end of the decline, a Secondary Test must bring out a much smaller amount of volume than at the Selling Climax. In addition, the price should meet support at a somewhat higher level than at the Selling Climax. This point is not as essential as is the lower volume. A successful Secondary Test may be accomplished at the level of the Selling Climax or even somewhat below it"[9] (as examples provided will illustrate).

Cases in which the Secondary Test penetrates the low of the Selling Climax carry a higher degree of risk than those where the ST holds above the low of the SC. As a result, price action subsequent to the ST becomes particularly important. If there is a lack of stabilization following a modest breach of the low of the SC, then the validity of the bottoming pattern would be called into question. Heavy volume on the Secondary Test as well as widening daily ranges on the decline would also suggest more work needs to be done on the downside before a valid bottoming formation gets underway.

After a successful ST is in place, the trading range defining the major market bottom can be identified. The nadir of the SC or ST defines the lower edge of the bottom formation, while the high of the Automatic Rally defines its upper edge. The initial ST may be followed by one or more subsequent STs, as the balance of Supply and Demand is determined and accumulation takes place.

In fact, these subsequent Secondary Tests often take on the form of one of two additional elements in the bottoming process: Springs and Shakeouts. As described in the Wyckoff Course,

> A Spring is designed to prove the stock's (market's) inability to decline. A Spring involves the penetration of a well defined trading range support level on low or moderate volume. The ideal case is when the penetration of the support is very small and the volume is very low. If a stock (market) is going to begin an important decline, it must break the bottom out of the trading range and do so on substantial volume. The Spring action shows that the stock (market) is trying to break down and failing badly. It is an important sign of strength usually followed by an aggressive rally.[10]

Another potential occurrence during the bottoming process is termed a Shakeout. Again, from Wyckoff,

> A Shakeout action is a sharp drop in price on heavy volume, which usually comes without warning and after an otherwise positive set of developments. It may bring a significant penetration of a prior support, although this is not a necessary feature, and there is almost always a speedy recovery.[11]

Although it may seem counterintuitive to call a Spring or a Shakeout a sign of strength, they demonstrate what the market is unable to do—sustain a break of support. That both a valid Spring and valid Shakeout are followed by what tends to be a significant rally underscores the fact that both developments serve to take stocks out of weak hands and redistribute those shares into strong hands, or those large operators who are positioning themselves for the impending bull market. It is those times when a significant rally fails to develop following a Spring or Shakeout that should cause the investor to beware, particularly if the apparent Spring or Shakeout occurs with a 90% Downside Day. Such a heavy wave of selling that is not followed by an equally dynamic recovery to back within what had appeared to be a developing trading range would imply the bottoming process has failed and the former bear market likely has further to run.

If a valid bottom is indeed in place, the end stages of the accumulation phase begin to emerge along with signs that sellers have exhausted their Supply and buyers have become the dominate players in the market. Subsequent phases of the bottoming process as well as the start of a new bull market are discussed in the following chapter. At present, however, we turn to a discussion regarding how Lowry's measures of the intermediate term trends of Supply and Demand, the Selling Pressure and Buying Power Indexes, add a quantifiable element to the identification of the end of a bear market and the initial stages of a major market bottom.

Lowry Indicators

Buying Power and Selling Pressure play important roles in the identification of major market tops and new bear markets, as discussed in Chapters 2 and 3. These indicators are also particularly useful in identifying major market bottoms and new bull markets, as they tend to provide signals that are more easily identifiable than the often subjective interpretation of price and volume behavior.

Put simply, during the formation of a major market low, Selling Pressure will peak in the early stages of the formation of a major market bottom, either at the same level as the Selling Climax or, at times, even earlier in the bottoming process. The peak in Selling Pressure and its subsequent decline implies a reduction in Supply, a key element in the formation of a major market low. While beyond the scope of this book, one of Lowry's Intermediate Term Buy Signals requires a particular point drop in the Selling Pressure Index, and this buy signal is often recorded within close proximity to major market lows.

The second element in the bottoming process is the emergence of enthusiastic and sustained investor Demand. This Demand is eventually evident in rising Buying Power throughout the formation of the range that defines the major market bottom. The combination of falling Selling Pressure and rising Buying Power, along with the development of 90% Upside and 90% Downside Days, help the investor recognize the various stages of the bottoming process which, in turn, allow for optimal entry of long positions early in what is likely to evolve into a new bull market. The following five examples of major market bottoms illustrate how the Wyckoff and Lowry methodologies mesh in determining when best to abandon the market on the short side and, instead, prepare for the eventual start of a new bull trend.

The Bottom of the 1968–1970 Bear Market

The formation of a major market top began in October 1968 and extended into May 1969. From the Last Point of Supply (LPSY) formed in May 1969, a bear market began that extended throughout the next year and shaved nearly 35% off the DJIA. While the ultimate low of that bear market occurred in May 1970, the bottoming process got underway in late March, which is illustrated in Figure 4.2.

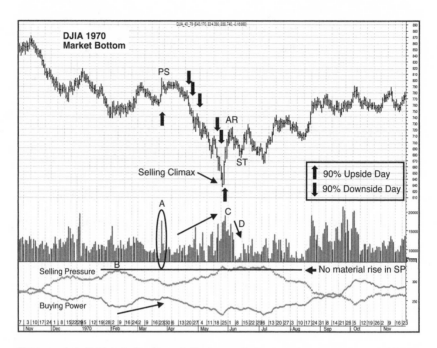

Charts created with Metastock, a Thomson Reuters product.

Figure 4.2   The initial phase of the 1970 major market bottom

The market experienced a brief, albeit powerful rally on March 25, 1970. This represented the first 90% Upside Day since the start of the bear market. In addition to representing a 90% Up Day, total volume surged (Point A). Thus, a change of character in the market was readily apparent, suggesting a potential point of Preliminary Support had been established. The PS was justified by the action of Selling Pressure, which had peaked about two months earlier in February (Point B) and had been trending lower since, implying a reduction in Supply. Over the same two-month period, Buying Power was trending higher, evidence of growing Demand.

However, the pain of the bear market was not over, as the point of PS gave way to another wave of Selling. This decline was accompanied by another turn lower in Buying Power and a commensurate move to the upside in Selling Pressure. It did not take long for the panic stage of the decline to develop, as roughly a month after the 90% Up Day/Preliminary Support, a series of five 90% Downside

Days occurred. This intense selling, or capitulation, took place amid heavy volume and wide daily ranges, key characteristics of the Selling Climax stage in the formation of a major market bottom.

While Selling Pressure was on the rise during the decline into the May 1970 bear market low, it is important to note that the level of Selling Pressure at this point was roughly the same as it had been back in early February 1970, prior to its decline during the rally into Preliminary Support. The lack of a meaningful expansion in Supply (Selling Pressure) during the decline into the Selling Climax supported the notion that a major market bottom was indeed under construction. If the bear market had additional legs on the downside, Selling Pressure should have experienced a notable expansion, breaking well above its February peak, suggesting Supply was not yet exhausted.

Further evidence that a major bottom was at hand occurred in the form of the May 27, 1970, 90% Upside Day, which occurred just two sessions after the final 90% Down Day of the Selling Climax. This series of 90% Down Days followed quickly by a 90% Up Day is classic evidence that prices had been discounted enough to draw in enthusiastic buyers. The 90% Up Day also provided clear evidence of the development of the next stage in the bottoming process: the Automatic Rally. The AR was the typical length of roughly one week and established the upper boundary of the bottoming formation (also referred to as the Creek, as discussed in Chapter 5).

Volume remained on the heavy side during the Automatic Reaction (Point C) but then dried up (Point D) as the market turned lower into what qualified as a Secondary Test of the Selling Climax. The diminished volume was a key element in determining the validity of the ST, as Selling Pressure had yet to noticeably contract from its recent highs while Buying Power was only marginally above its late May 1970 low. However, at this point in the bottom structure, long commitments are not yet warranted. Therefore, if the bottoming formation fails, investors' capital would not have been compromised.

While the market does not appear to be gearing up for a new bull market at this stage of the bottoming process, investors should be mindful of the developments that transpire in the days and weeks ahead, as the final stages of the bottoming process were to come.

The Bottom of the 1973–1974 Bear Market

Following the establishment of the January 1973 market top, the equity market rolled over into a bear market that persisted until an initial low was established in October 1974. This 21-month bear market resulted in a 44% decline in the DJIA. Although the bear market was interrupted by a roughly a two-month advance in August–October 1973 that resulted in a gain of nearly 16%, there was a lack of evidence indicating that the preceding bear market had run its course. Indeed, following that run higher, the market reversed in late October and by mid-November 1974 was sitting at new bear market lows.

Evidence that a sustainable low was close at hand, however, did appear nearly ten months later, in August 1974 (Figure 4.3). This evidence was in the form of a brief three-day advance that should have caught the eye of the astute investor, given the strong Demand exhibited on August 7, 1974. Although this session did not qualify as a 90% Upside Day, it came very close, with Up Volume representing 89.3% of total Up/Down Volume and Points Gained representing 89.4% of Points Gained plus Points Lost. This was the strongest Demand exhibited by the market since the second trading day of 1974. And though mediocre volume on the advance (Point A) and its failure to qualify as a bona fide 90% Upside Day were reasons for caution, evidence of a possible point of Preliminary Support was in place. Therefore, investors should have remained alert for the appearance of additional signs of the bottoming process.

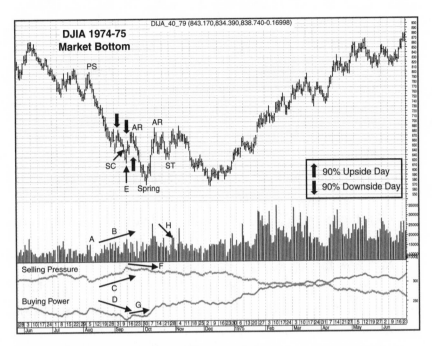

Charts created with Metastock, a Thomson Reuters product.

Figure 4.3   The initial phase of the 1974-1975 major market bottom

Additional signs did appear, as the subsequent move to new bear market lows eventually gave way to panic selling, as two 90% Down Days developed within the span of seven trading sessions. Although volume did increase during the move lower (Point B), there was none of the typical heavy turnover seen during the Selling Climax phase. However, Selling Pressure did experience a rather steep increase during the SC phase (Point C), while Buying Power was in an equally steep decline (Point D), implying stocks were being dumped at all cost, while buyers remained on the sidelines, unwilling rush in and grab up the bargains.

The mood quickly changed, however, as Demand resurfaced September 16, 1974, with the market forming an upside reversal day (the market makes a lower-low but reverses to end the day higher, Point E). The subsequent advance persisted for the next three sessions, culminating with a 90% Upside Day on September 19. Strong volume on the upside reversal day combined with the subsequent 90% Upside Day provided persuasive evidence that the next phase of the bottoming process, the Automatic Rally, had indeed taken place.

In Figure 4.3, the Automatic Rally was followed by a turn lower that resulted in a break below the low of the SC. This sell-off occurred on relatively moderate volume. Therefore, it met the definition of a potential Spring, as volume would had to have been heavier to qualify as a Shakeout. The validity of the Spring was then confirmed with the subsequent rally, which qualified as a second Automatic Rally on heavy volume.

Note how the actions of Buying Power and Selling Pressure supported the notion that the drop below the low of the Selling Climax represented a stage in the bottoming process and not the start of another leg lower in the preceding bear market. Specifically, as the market tumbled during the Spring action, Selling Pressure was trending lower (Point F) while Buying Power was moving higher (Point G). Had the market been embarking on another leg lower in the primary downtrend, Selling Pressure should have moved above the peak established during the Selling Climax, while Buying Power resumed its contraction.

The second Automatic Reaction was then followed by another turn lower on declining volume (Point H). The light volume and stabilization of the market in the same vicinity as the low of the SC implied a valid Secondary Test had been established. Further confirmation was provided by Buying Power and Selling Pressure, as the former continued to trend higher while the latter extended its decline, implying Supply was continuing to dry up while Demand was gradually gaining the upper hand. Although the bottoming formation had further to progress, enough solid evidence was in place, by late October 1974, to indicate a valid major bottom was indeed forming.

The Bottom of the 1981–1982 Bear Market

The 1980–1981 bull market topped in April 1981, and the subsequent bear market did not reach its final low until nearly 16 months later in August 1982, after the DJIA had declined 24%. Although the ultimate low of the bear market was not established until August, the bottoming process actually started taking shape in late January 1982.

During this time, the market embarked on its first 90% Upside Day of the ongoing bear market, implying a level of Preliminary Support had potentially been established. In addition to the strong wave of buying, volume also notably increased on the 90% Up Day, which is evident in Figure 4.4 (Point A). Finally, Selling Pressure had peaked months prior, back in late September 1981 (Point B), and was in the midst of a steady move lower, indicating diminishing Supply. This contraction in Supply was accompanied by steadily increasing intermediate term Demand, as indicated by the rise in Buying Power that had been underway also since late September 1981 (Point C).

When the potential point of Preliminary Support was in place, the market turned lower, falling to new bear market lows. This renewed leg to the downside was accompanied by the development of one 90% Downside Day as well as a steady increase in volume (Point D), sufficient evidence of the development of a Selling Climax. The SC was followed by a dramatic upside reversal day (lower-low/higher-close, Point E) that occurred on heavy volume, qualifying as an Automatic Reaction. The Automatic Reaction proved brief, as did the subsequent pullback (Point F), which qualified as a Secondary Test given the drop in volume. Although the aforementioned developments occurred within a rather compressed span of time, the volume patterns and the ongoing downtrend in Selling Pressure as well as the uptrend in Buying Power suggested that the pieces of a valid major market bottom were falling into place. However, major bottoms do typically take longer to play out and, as is discussed in the next chapter, there was some additional base building on tap in the coming months prior to the eventual breakout that led to the start of the next bull market.

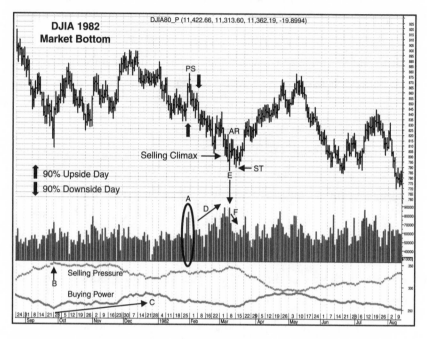

Charts created with Metastock, a Thomson Reuters product.

Figure 4.4   The initial phase of the 1982 major market bottom

The Bottom of the 2000–2003 Bear Market

As many readers of this book will remember, the 2000–2003 bear market was a painful event that resulted in a 78% drop in the NAS-DAQ Comp., as high flying Internet issues imploded. Other major market indexes did not escape the turmoil but experienced less of a decline, with the DJIA dropping about 38% over a period of 33 months. After what seemed like a never-ending drop in equity prices, the market finally showed some signs of promise in early July 2002, as seen in Figure 4.5, as the first 90% Upside Day since March 2000 developed, thereby causing astute investors to take notice and suggesting a potential point of Preliminary Support had been established.

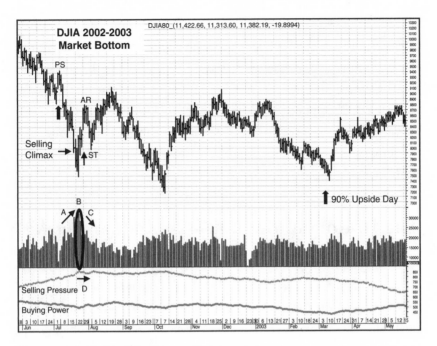

Charts created with Metastock, a Thomson Reuters product.

Figure 4.5   The initial phase of the 2002-2003 major market bottom

The strength exhibited in early July, however, proved short-lived, as the market turned lower, establishing new bear market lows. Volume surged during this move to new lows (Point A) while the daily ranges expanded, evidence a Selling Climax was indeed underway. Prices apparently dropped low enough to elicit enthusiastic investor Demand, as the market experienced a strong about-face, accompanied by volume that was even stronger (Point B) than that which accompanied the Selling Climax. This apparent Automatic Rally culminated with the development of another 90% Upside Day which, in this case, apparently was enough to at least temporarily exhaust Demand, as the market soon turned lower.

This pullback occurred on diminished volume (Point C), suggesting a Secondary Test of the Selling Climax was underway. Just as in the preceding example of the bottom of the 1981–1982 bear market, these initial stages of the development of a major market bottom played out over a relatively short period of time, implying that, although the pieces of a bear market low appeared to be falling into place, there was likely still work to be done in the months ahead, and new buying at this point in the bottoming process was not yet warranted. This final point is especially important given that Selling Pressure had not yet established a sustained downtrend, having just recently peaked during the establishment of the SC and subsequent ST (Point D).

The Bottom of the 2007–2009 Bear Market

The final major market bottom to be reviewed in this chapter is the most recent one established prior to the publication of this book, the bottom of the 2007–2009 bear market. Many factors led to this bear market, the worst since 1929. A housing market bubble, credit crisis, and misuse of leverage were just some of the contributing factors leading to a bear market that pushed the DJIA down nearly 54% over a span of 17 months.

Evidence of the potential beginning of the end of the bear market occurred in September 2008 with the development of a 90% Upside Day, as can be seen in Figure 4.6. This had been the first 90% Upside Day since April 2008. The 90% Upside Day that occurred in April 2008 was quickly proven an invalid point of Preliminary Support, given the absence of the development of a subsequent Selling Climax and a lack of heavy volume.

On the September 2008 90% Upside Day, however, volume noticeably increased (Point A), suggesting a potential change of character for the market. Selling then quickly resumed, and volume steadily increased (Point B) as the market produced four 90% Down Days in the span of nine trading sessions and fell to new bear market lows. This breakdown suggested that in addition to forming a valid level of Preliminary Support in September, the market had also experienced a Selling Climax during the decline into early October.

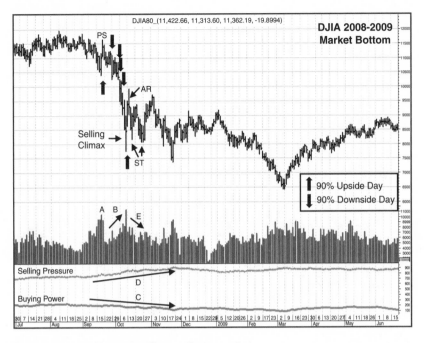

Charts created with Metastock, a Thomson Reuters product.

Figure 4.6   The initial phase of the 2008-2009 major market bottom

The bottoming process was by no means near an end, however, as the trends of Buying Power (Point C) and Selling Pressure (Point D) implied Supply remained a dominant force driving the market. Nonetheless, the bottoming process outlined by the Wyckoff methodology appeared to be in place, given the subsequent Automatic Rally in mid-October 2008. That Automatic Rally was followed by back-to-back Secondary Tests that occurred on diminishing volume (Point E), implying a successful bottoming formation was indeed underway.

However, as with the preceding example of the 2000–2003 bear market bottom, Selling Pressure had yet to establish a readily identifiable peak, warning that although the bottoming process appeared to be underway, more work likely needed to be done in the coming months, and if a valid bottom was indeed in place, Selling Pressure's movements would eventually indicate a weakening of the intermediate term trend of Supply.

Endnotes

[1] "Identifying Bear Market Bottoms and New Bull Markets," Paul F. Desmond, 2002.

[2] *Wyckoff Stock Market Course; Volume One,* The Stock Market Institute, Phoenix, AZ, 33.

[3] *Wyckoff Stock Market Course; Volume One,* The Stock Market Institute, Phoenix, AZ, 33.

[4] *Wyckoff Stock Market Course; Volume One,* The Stock Market Institute, Phoenix, AZ, 34.

[5] "Identifying Bear Market Bottoms and New Bull Markets," Paul F. Desmond, 2002.

[6] "Identifying Bear Market Bottoms and New Bull Markets," Paul F. Desmond, 2002.

[7] "Identifying Bear Market Bottoms and New Bull Markets," Paul F. Desmond, 2002.

[8] *Wyckoff Stock Market Course; Volume One,* The Stock Market Institute, Phoenix, AZ, 34.

[9] *Wyckoff Stock Market Course; Volume One,* The Stock Market Institute, Phoenix, AZ, 34.

[10] *Wyckoff Stock Market Course; Volume One,* The Stock Market Institute, Phoenix, AZ, 37.

[11] *Wyckoff Stock Market Course; Volume One,* The Stock Market Institute, Phoenix, AZ, 38.

5

How Major Market Bottoms Form: Part II, Accumulation and Breakout

The initial phase of the development of a major market bottom involves the latter stages of the bear market and the very early stages of the accumulation process. At this point in the process, however, selling has not yet been fully exhausted, as few investors believe with conviction that a bottom is actually in place. In fact, it is near the end stages of a bear market when the financial press is typically filled with articles projecting a deepened and protracted decline for equities in the weeks, if not months, ahead. This feeling of continued despair on the part of equity investors is often bolstered by economic data which, at this point in the bottoming process, still indicates an economy nowhere close to embarking on a sustainable recovery. Various investor surveys often confirm widespread despair. In fact, a survey conducted by the American Association of Individual Investors as of March 5, 2009, indicated that 70% of investors considered themselves "bears." This reading of overwhelming bearishness occurred within a week of the final low of the 2007–2009 bear market. As L.M. Lowry used to say, "It begins to get light from the very darkest hour of night."

The second phase of the bottoming process includes the completion of the distribution process, an acceleration of the accumulation process, and the ascent into a new bull market. As was the case with the initial phase of a major market bottom, a combination of the Wyckoff and Lowry methodologies can greatly aid in identifying the end stages of the bottoming process which, in turn, should allow an investor to reap the benefits of the "meat" of the subsequent bull market.

Idealized Major Market Bottoming Pattern (Part II)

In Chapter 4, "How Major Market Bottoms Form: Part I, Panic and Capitulation," the bottoming process included a discussion of the point of Preliminary Support (PS) and the subsequent Selling Climax (SC), Automatic Reaction and Secondary Test (ST). The ST may not represent an isolated event, as can be seen in Figure 5.1. Numerous STs and/or Springs and Shakeouts, also discussed in Chapter 4, may occur as stocks are moving from weak into strong hands.

Figure 5.1   Wyckoff's key points for identifying a major market bottom

Rallies that follow Springs, Shakeouts and tests of these events tend to be particularly important. After having failed in an attempt to move to new bear market lows, the market should be, as stated in the Wyckoff Course:

...in a position to make a significant rally usually over a relatively short period of time and accompanied by a substantial
increase in the level of volume. A rally of this nature coming
at this point represents a Sign of Strength (SOS), as shown
in Figure 5.1. Such a move is important here because it
adds further confirmation to what the Spring (or Shakeout)
action suggests. At the Spring (or Shakeout or test of either)
a stock (market) is saying it cannot go down. When the Sign
of Strength is added, it is as though the stock (market) is
saying "I told you so," and indicating what it can do
instead."[1]

Sign of Strength Rallies often, but not always, result in a breakout
from the sideways trading range that represents the major bottom
formation. The upper edge of this range is referred to as the Creek.
According to Wyckoff, "A Creek is an imaginary line that winds its
way across the top action of the trading range."[2]

The breakout above the Creek is termed the Jump Across the
Creek:

A Jump Across the Creek is a sharp quick rise in price generally accomplished in one or several days that propels the stock
(market) up and out of the trading range. To be effective, the
surge in price must be accompanied by a surge in volume as
well. There is no set amount by which the top of the trading
range must be broken for the action to qualify as a Jump
Across the Creek. To provide the optimal trading opportunity, however, the penetration should be several points.[3]

Typically, the ill-informed investor chooses to initiate purchases
on a Sign of Strength rally, whether it is confined to the boundaries of
the trading range or results in a breakout from the range and effec-
tively represents the Jump Across the Creek. However, this action is
not optimal, because it entails buying on an advance, which carries
with it a heightened degree of risk. Again from Wyckoff, "Although
the urge to buy on the aggressive showing of a Sign of Strength rally is
strong, it must be controlled in favor of the next reaction, which is
known as the Last Point of Support (LPS)."[4]

Just as the bottoming process can contain several Automatic Reactions, Springs, Shakeouts and Secondary Tests, several Last Points of Support may also develop. However, the LPS an investor should be most concerned with is that which occurs following a Jump Across the Creek. This particular Last Point of Support is known by its own distinctive moniker in Wyckoff terminology, the Back Up to the Edge of the Creek. Although traditional Wyckoff analysis notes several areas during the bottoming formation that can be used to initiate long positions, for simplicity's sake (and to offer a relatively low risk entry point), the ideal buy point is considered the pullback representing the Back Up to the Edge of the Creek. As the following examples illustrate, this final LPS might not result in an actual retest of the Creek. In fact, the Wyckoff Course states,

> ...relative strength is implied if a reaction meets support at or above the halfway point of the previous rally. If the volume is greatly reduced from that of the previous rally and if support is being met at or above the half way point of the rally, it is reasonable to conclude that a Last Point of Support (also qualified as a Back Up to the Edge of the Creek) is being experienced. Therefore, it is justifiable to take a long position.[5]

Whatever the amount of the preceding rally is retraced, the Back Up to the Edge of the Creek should be readily identifiable, given the substantial decrease in volume that occurs along with it.

Lowry Indicators

In the final phase of the bottoming process, 90% Upside Days play an important role. Often advances that represent Sign of Strength rallies or the rebound following a Last Point of Support will come in the form of one or more 90% Up Days or back-to-back 80% Upside Days (which act as a proxy for a 90% Up Day, according to the Lowry Analysis). While the development of 90% Upside Days aid greatly in the identification of key areas in the bottoming process, the action of Selling Pressure is also particularly important. Although the following examples illustrate that Buying Power does not always develop a sustained uptrend until late in the bottoming process, it is a requirement that Selling Pressure fails to expand or, in some cases, steadily declines throughout the majority of the life of the bottom formation. It is the lack of expansion in Selling Pressure that is key to the bottoming process. Lowry's history shows that bull markets rarely begin until well after the Selling Pressure Index has started to contract from its bear market high, providing strong evidence that the desire to sell has been exhausted.

What follows is a discussion of the second phase of the bear market bottom process for each of the five major bottoms discussed in Chapter 4. The culmination of distribution, the acceleration of accumulation, and the beginning of the actual bull trend are illustrated in each example.

The Bottom of the 1968–1970 Bear Market

We ended the previous chapter's discussion of the bottom of the 1968–1970 bear market with mention of the development of a low volume Secondary Test of the May 1970 Selling Climax. This ST, as shown in Figure 5.2, was followed by a rebound rally that tested the high of the preceding Automatic Rally (Point A). This advance was accompanied by volume that was much lower (Point B) than that on the initial Automatic Rally, thereby disqualifying the advance as a Sign of Strength rally.

The market then once again turned lower, dropping marginally below the low of the initial ST on continued light volume. At the low of the subsequent ST, Selling Pressure was essentially at the same level as at the low of the Selling Climax (Point C). Although the Index had yet to contract, the lack of expansion in Selling Pressure relative to its May 1970 level implied a potentially valid bottom formation was at hand.

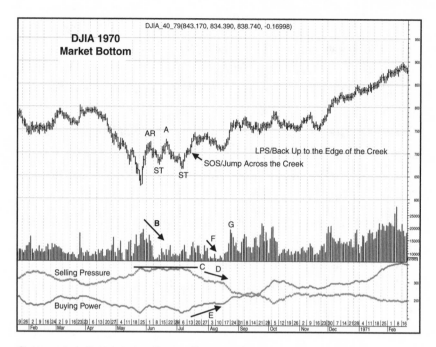

Charts created with Metastock, a Thomson Reuters product.

Figure 5.2   The final phase of the 1970 major market bottom

Following the early July 1970 Secondary Test, another rally ensued. Although volume experienced only a modest expansion during the latter stage of this advance, Selling Pressure experienced a notable contraction (Point D) while Buying Power (Point E) experienced a commensurate expansion—thus evidence a Sign of Strength rally was at hand. A loosely drawn line from the top of the Automatic Rally (AR) and subsequent mid-June rebound rally high (Point A) formed the Creek, and the Sign of Strength rally resulted in a Jump Across the Creek.

This advance was followed by a consolidation that devolved into a pullback on extremely low volume (Point F). Note that despite the decline in the market, Selling Pressure continued to trend lower while Buying Power continued to rise. These factors, combined with the light volume, implied a LPS had been formed and, given its close proximity to the Creek, also qualified as a Back Up to the Edge of the

Creek. It is at this point, on the low volume Back Up to the Edge of the Creek, where the initiation of long positions is warranted, as solid evidence of the completion of a major market bottom was in place. Note on the rally following the Last Point of Support, volume exploded (Point G), further confirmation that a new bull market was underway.

The Bottom of the 1973–1975 Bear Market

In our discussion of the bottom of the 1973–1975 bear market, we left off with the development of a second Automatic Reaction followed by a low volume Secondary Test that bottomed in the same vicinity as the mid-September 1974 Selling Climax. During these developments, Selling Pressure was trending lower (Point A) while Buying Power was in the midst of an even stronger uptrend (Point B), evidence that distribution was diminishing and accumulation was taking place.

We pick up with another rebound rally that halts in the same vicinity as the prior Automatic Rallies (Point C), as shown in Figure 5.3. This rally occurs on slightly heavier volume (Point D) than that which accompanied the preceding Secondary Test, a constructive development. While the three consecutive rally highs were forming the Creek, the bottoming process was by no means complete, as the market subsequently turned lower and declined all the way back to the low of the initial Spring. Despite the troubling price action and the development of two 90% Downside Days during this decline, volume was exceptionally light during the month-long sell-off (Point E), indicating that when the market appeared to stabilize, what transpired could be labeled a valid second Spring. Supporting the notion that a bottom formation was indeed still intact were Buying Power and Selling Pressure, as Selling Pressure remained below its peak established during the Selling Climax while Buying Power was holding well above its equivalent low (Point F).

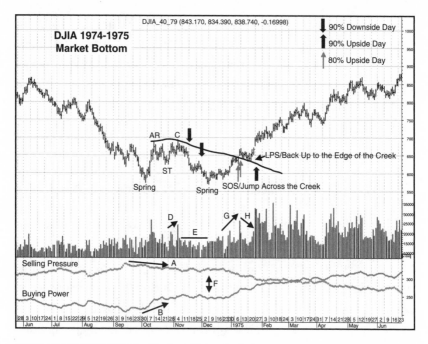

Figure 5.3   The final phase of the 1974-1975 major market bottom

The market then, once again, turned to the upside and exhibited a clear Sign of Strength rally in the form of back-to-back 80% Upside Days, which according to Lowry Research, act as a proxy for a 90% Upside Day. This burst of strength also occurred on expanding volume (Point G) and resulted in a Jump Across the Creek. When that rally culminated in early January 1975, a low volume pullback (Point H) ensued that stabilized above the loosely drawn Creek. The pullback on light volume implied the development of a Last Point of Support (LPS) that also qualified as a Back Up Against the Creek, thereby offering a buying opportunity into a bull market which extended into 1976. Note that as the rally got underway, volume expanded dramatically, and a 90% Upside Day developed, adding further confirmation to the notion that a new bull market was in place.

The Bottom of the 1981–1982 Bear Market

The first phase of the bottom of the 1981–1982 bear market occurred over a compressed period of time, with the Selling Climax, Automatic Reaction and Secondary Test all occurring within a span of less than two weeks, as noted by Point A in Figure 5.4. Despite the compressed time frame, the volume patterns as well as the ongoing downtrend in Selling Pressure (Point B) and uptrend in Buying Power (Point C) suggested that the pieces of a valid major market bottom were falling into place. However, because major bottoms typically take longer than a couple of weeks to play out, the well-informed investor should have been anticipating additional base building in the months ahead.

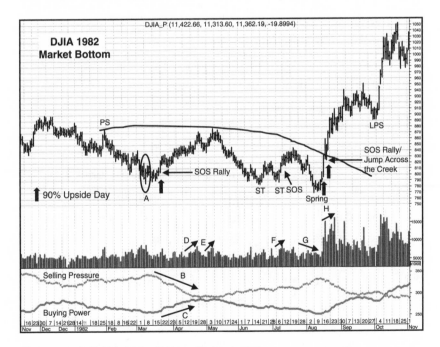

Charts created with Metastock, a Thomson Reuters product.

Figure 5.4   The final phase of the 1982 major market bottom

And additional base building did indeed occur, but not before a Sign of Strength rally developed that may have left some believing the bottoming process was complete. This Sign of Strength rally occurred on modest expansion in volume over that on the Secondary Test and included a 90% Upside Day on March 22, 1982.

This rally persisted for more than a month and was accompanied by a sharp contraction in Selling Pressure as well as a steep rise in Buying Power. However, despite these constructive developments and the expansion in volume (Point D) that occurred at the latter stage of the advance, the market failed to overcome the high of the point of Preliminary Support (PS). Then after a brief pullback, another rally occurred, again with expanding volume (Point E), yet once again the advance failed at precisely the same level. The dual failed rallies suggested Supply remained a factor and, as a result, the bottoming process was not yet complete.

Indeed, the market turned lower and sold off over the next month and a half, falling back to test the low of the Selling Climax formed more than three months earlier in March 1982. While Selling Pressure climbed higher during this time period, its longer term downtrend dating back to September 1981 remained in place, implying that, despite the pullback, the market appeared unlikely to roll over into a renewed bear trend.

Following this establishment of another ST, a brief rebound ensued but was quickly followed by another pullback that established a third ST of the bear market bottom. The market then appeared to finally be rejuvenated, as a rally developed on a clear expansion in volume (Point F), implying the development of a Sign of Strength rally. However, the bottoming process was still playing out, as the Sign of Strength rally topped in mid-July 1982 and the market dropped to new bear market lows in August.

This apparent breakdown might have led some to believe a new leg to the downside had begun, but there was evidence to the contrary. First, volume declined during the breakdown (Point G), suggesting new Supply was not coming on the market. In addition, although Selling Pressure rose sharply during the late July/early

August sell-off, Selling Pressure's longer term downtrend remained intact as it formed a lower high than that established during the Selling Climax. Given the diminished volume and the modest break below the low of the SC, a potential Spring was in place.

This Spring, as well as the culmination of the bottoming process, was confirmed with the subsequent Sign of Strength rally that occurred on a surge in volume (Point H) and included the development of two 90% Upside Days. At the same time, Selling Pressure dove while Buying Power experienced a commensurate expansion. The Sign of Strength rally also served as a Jump Across the Creek, and the subsequent advance extended into late September.

A modest pullback amid diminished volume did eventually develop, indicating a Last Point of Support (LPS) was forming. This LPS retraced less than half the preceding Sign of Strength rally. As previously noted, if support is met at or above the half way point of the Sign of Strength rally, it is reasonable to conclude that an LPS (also qualifying as a Back Up to the Edge of the Creek) was underway. Therefore, initiating long positions was warranted. And any new long positions, although entered a good distance above the ultimate bear market low, would have reaped the spectacular gains of the 1982–2000 secular bull market.

The Bottom of the 2000–2003 Bear Market

As was the case for the bottom of the 1981–1982 bear market, the initial stages of the 2002–2003 major market bottom played out over a relatively short period of time, as outlined in the preceding chapter. But although the pieces of a bear market low appeared to be falling into place, there was likely still more work to be done in the bottoming process over the months ahead. This was particularly true given that Selling Pressure did not establish a sustained downtrend during the initial phase of the bottoming process.

We pick up the 2002–2003 bottom with the Secondary Test of the Selling Climax, as shown in Figure 5.5. The ST was followed by another move to the upside that surpassed the high of the Automatic Rally but was not accompanied by any noticeable expansion in volume (Point A). Given the lackluster volume, chances the market was in the midst of a sustained move higher appeared rather slim.

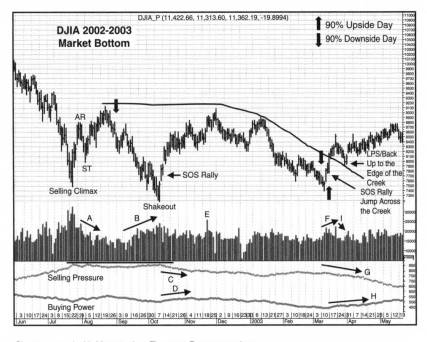

Charts created with Metastock, a Thomson Reuters product.

Figure 5.5   The final phase of the 2002-2003 major market bottom

Indeed, the market turned lower, and though the decline quickly produced a 90% Downside Day in early September, this brief surge of selling served to exhaust Supply only temporarily, as the market quickly resumed its decline and eventually broke below the low of the Selling Climax. Given the break of the low of the SC and the steady increase in volume (Point B) that occurred during the decline, the market appeared to be either in the process of resuming the bear market or completing a Shakeout. A Shakeout, as discussed in the previous chapter, is one of the potential developments that occurs in the bottoming process as stocks are moving from weak to strong hands.

Price action and volume alone would have made it difficult to decipher which path the market would ultimately take. However, the action of Selling Pressure lends an important element to the analysis, in that it did not surpass its July peak during the Shakeout. This lower high, relative to that established on the SC, implied that despite the market's break to new lows, the amount of Supply coming on the market had diminished, an important development indicating the market was indeed still in the bottoming process. Had the bear market resumed, Selling Pressure should have confirmed the increase in Supply with a move to new highs in its former uptrend.

During the subsequent rebound, which confirmed the establishment of a valid Shakeout, volume remained strong, signaling a Sign of Strength (SOS) rally. During this time, Selling Pressure (Point C) also began notably to contract while Buying Power (Point D) expanded, further evidence that the bottoming process remained underway. The Sign of Strength rally extended into the latter part of November 2002 and, while volume had tapered off from its levels during the beginning of the Sign of Strength rally, it surged as the market rallied toward the high of the August 2002 advance. The surge in volume (Point E) and failure to break above resistance is an example of one of Wyckoff's Rules: Effort vs. Result. In this case, the heavy volume (Effort) failed to elicit an equally strong price move (Result). The fact resistance was able to remain intact suggested the bottoming process was not yet complete.

Indeed, the subsequent turn lower persisted for more than three months and brought the market down to test a support zone now defined by the Selling Climax and the Shakeout. The lack of a notable expansion in volume during the decline and the continued downtrend in Selling Pressure as the pullback progressed supported the theory that the market was in the process of forming a Spring. Just ahead of the final low of the Spring, the market formed a 90% Downside Day, signaling a strong surge in selling. Apparently, this surge in selling was enough to rejuvenate Demand, as the subsequent rebound rally contained a 90% Upside Day, evidence of enthusiastic buying. The 90% Upside Day, along with a rise in volume (Point F), accelerated decline in Selling Pressure (Point G) and increase in Buying Power (Point H), all implied a valid Sign of Strength rally was underway and the bottoming process was near completion.

The Sign of Strength rally resulted in a Jump Across the Creek, with the Creek loosely drawn across the highs established during the bottom formation. After the Sign of Strength rally peaked in mid-March, the market turned lower on diminished volume, suggesting the development of a Last Point of Support. This pullback also qualified as a Back Up to the Edge of the Creek, thereby offering a rather low risk opportunity to buy into the early stages of what evolved into a new bull market that would persist over the next four years.

The Bottom of the 2007–2009 Bear Market

The bottom of the 2007–2009 bear market represented a particularly volatile time in stock market history, as the proliferation of 90% Days in Figure 5.6 illustrates. The increase in 90% Days during the bear market as well as during the bottoming process appears largely due to the abolition of the Uptick Rule in July 2007. The Uptick Rule required that a security be shorted on an uptick in price. According to the U.S. Securities and Exchange Commission, a listed security may be sold short (A) at a price above the price at which the immediately preceding sale was effected (plus tick), or (B) at the last sale price if it is higher than the last different price (zero-plus tick). This rule was overturned in July 2007, resulting in more frequent 90% Days. While their increased frequency has, in some cases, diminished their utility, 90% Days did play a critical role in the formation of the 2009 market bottom, as the following example illustrates.

We pick up with the market in 2008 after back-to-back Secondary Tests that occurred on diminished volume relative to that on the

Automatic Rally, implying a successful bottoming formation was indeed underway. The advance following the second ST contained a 90% Upside Day. This implied strong Demand was coming into the market, but the lack of evidence of a top in Selling Pressure (Point A) and the continued downtrend in Buying Power (Point B) suggested the bottoming process was not yet in the end stages.

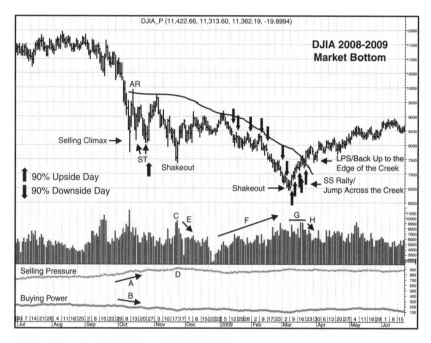

Charts created with Metastock, a Thomson Reuters product.

Figure 5.6   The final phase of the 2008-2009 major market bottom

This rebound proved temporary, as the market rolled over and broke below the low of the Selling Climax. Given the spike in volume (Point C) and support break, this price action was labeled a Shakeout. Note that during the decline into the Shakeout, Selling Pressure moved to a new rally peak (Point D), which was further evidence that while a bottom appeared to be forming, more work was still to come.

The market stabilized relatively quickly following the Shakeout and the subsequent advance, on diminished volume (Point E), stopping short of the preceding rally highs. The market then embarked on another move to the downside, and this pullback occurred on steadily increasing volume (Point F). The urgency of the selling during this pullback was evident, given the development of seven 90% Downside Days over a relatively short period of time. Despite the panic selling and the decisive break below the 2008 lows, the uptrend in Selling Pressure did not reassert itself. Specifically, Selling Pressure's peak in March 2009 was 20 points below its peak in November 2008. Thus, a potential second Shakeout, not a new leg lower in the bear market, appeared at hand.

This Shakeout was then confirmed by the subsequent rally in which volume remained heavy (Point G) and five 90% Upside Days in close succession developed. This strong burst of Demand clearly represented a Sign of Strength rally that also qualified as a Jump Across the Creek, with the Creek being drawn roughly across the highs established during the bottoming formation. Clearly, the positioning of the Creek is up to one's own interpretation. The key elements to recognize are the development of the Sign of Strength rally and the subsequent Last Point of Support.

In the case of the 2008–2009 bottom, the LPS was a brief event that occurred during the latter part of March 2009 amid diminished volume (Point H) relative to that on the preceding rally. It also represented a Back Up to the Edge of the Creek that completed only a modest retracement of the preceding advance, indicating positive relative strength. While Selling Pressure had yet to noticeably contract, its longer term downtrend dating from November 2008 was never violated during the bottoming process or in the subsequent advance. As a result, new buying at the establishment of the LPS would have been warranted and, given the extent of the subsequent bull market, which remains intact as of this writing, rewards reaped from these purchases should have proven substantial.

The final chapter of this book delves deeper into the developments that occurred in the primary uptrend, as well as in Buying

Power and Selling Pressure, during the months following the establishment of the March 2009 low. There were several interesting developments as the trend progressed, some of which undoubtedly caused some nail biting. However, given the trends in Buying Power and Selling Pressure, as well as positive trends in other important ancillary indicators, the current bull market still appears alive and well.

Endnotes

[1] *Wyckoff Stock Market Course; Volume One*, The Stock Market Institute, Phoenix, AZ, 37.

[2] *Wyckoff Stock Market Course; Volume One*, The Stock Market Institute, Phoenix, AZ, 39.

[3] *Wyckoff Stock Market Course; Volume One*, The Stock Market Institute, Phoenix, AZ, 39-40.

[4] *Wyckoff Stock Market Course; Volume One*, The Stock Market Institute, Phoenix, AZ, 37.

[5] *Wyckoff Stock Market Course; Volume One*, The Stock Market Institute, Phoenix, AZ, 40.

Part II _____

Combining a Wyckoff-Lowry Analysis with Other Tools for Timing Major Market Tops and Bottoms

In Part II, the authors bring other analytical tools into play for identifying major market turning points. These tools include Point and Figure Counts, Advance-Decline Lines, and other measures of market strength and weakness. In addition, special consideration is given to the 2000 market top, due to its unique characteristics.

6

Building a Cause: How R.D. Wyckoff Uses Point and Figure Charts to Establish Price Targets

Thus far, we have described how Wyckoff's laws of Supply and Demand and Effort vs. Result are useful tools in helping identify major market tops and bottoms. There is a third law, Cause and Effect, that is also an important component of a Wyckoff analysis. Briefly put, the Law of Cause and Effect states there is an equal and corresponding effect for every cause. In today's terms, this law is often stated as "the bigger the base the bigger the rally." For purposes of identifying major market tops and bottoms, the Law of Cause and Effect is useful in setting rough targets for bull and bear markets. For example, as prior chapters have illustrated, a new bull market is typically preceded by a period in which the major price indexes move in a roughly-defined trading range. This generally sideways pattern is termed the *base*, or *basing pattern*. This basing pattern is used to calculate the possible extent of the ensuing bull market. That is, when the basing period prior to a new bull market has been completed, a rough target range as to the extent of the ensuing market uptrend can be calculated from the extent, or width, of the base. Thus, indications of a bull market top (Buying Climax, Sign of Weakness, Break through the Ice, for example) that occur within the target range established by this base would, therefore, carry a higher probability of signaling the bull market is, indeed, over. The same technique of measuring the width of a topping pattern in a bull market is used for

103

establishing a potential range for the ensuing bear market. Does it work? We let the reader judge this based on the illustrations that follow. First, though, we need to quickly review the tools needed to establish a target range, beginning with the charting technique.

Point and Figure Charts

Technical analysis uses many different forms of charts. Vertical bar charts and point and figure charts are two of the most basic. Unlike vertical charts, which have two axes (one for price, the other for time), point and figure charts have only one axis, the one for price. There are many excellent texts that cover the construction and interpretation of point and figure charts, so we limit ourselves to only a rudimentary discussion before going into their applications in establishing price targets for bull and bear markets.

There are two primary elements to a point and figure chart: box size and reversal amount. For the most part, the prices plotted utilize a trading day's high or low. The charts are plotted on graph paper with boxes that form a grid. These boxes are then given price values: 1 point, 5 points, 10 points, and so on. The size of the box is typically dependent on the price of the security being charted. For instance, a one point per box chart might be appropriate for a stock trading in low single or double digits; however, using a one point box when charting a high priced stock such as Apple or Google would require reams of graph paper. Consequently, a large box size, likely in the range of 5 or 10 points per box, is more useful. The same applies when charting a market index. A point and figure chart of the S&P 500, for example, might use a box size of 20 points per box, while a box size of 100 points would likely be more applicable for charting the DJ Industrial Average.

The second element in a point and figure chart, the reversal amount, has changed over the years. Wyckoff, in his original analysis, typically used a one-box reversal. In current usage, however, each column must contain at least two boxes. That is, a reversal on the point and figure chart would be triggered by a change of two boxes. Thus a price change that reverses price by only one box would not be enough to begin a new column. Up to this day, purists consider the one-box reversal method as the only "valid" means of constructing a point and figure chart. For readers interested in more detail on this original method of point and figure charting, a good start is with *The Point and Figure Method of Anticipating Stock Price Movements* by Victor de Villiers, published in 1933, but available today in a reprinted edition by Marketplace Publishing. Another good source is *Study Helps in Point and Figure Technique* by Alexander Wheelan, published in 1954.

The three-box reversal method, which has arguably become the most popular form of point and figure charting today, was introduced in 1947 by Earl Blumenthal with his Chartcraft Service.[1] Under this method, all price movement that encompasses less than three boxes is ignored. Over the years, the greater ease with which the three-box reversal can be plotted and the fact these charts can be constructed from data in the newspaper or from online sources has resulted in this method becoming regarded as the standard. It is not the purpose of this book to delve into the advantages or disadvantages of one-box versus three-box reversals. Each method has its strengths and weaknesses. For our purposes and for clarity of illustration, the examples used in this chapter are all based on the three-box reversal method.

Construction of a Point and Figure Chart

Constructing a basic bar chart of price movement requires drawing a straight line on a graph connecting the high and low price for the day, completing the process with a small horizontal line at the level of the closing price. Voila! You're done (unless, of course, volume is also being plotted, which requires another vertical line plotted below the price bar). A point and figure chart, however, with its columns of Xs and Os can appear more intimidating. However, once learned, plotting a point and figure chart is a relatively quick and easy operation.

The basic point and figure chart consists of alternating columns of Xs and Os, with advancing prices represented by Xs and declining prices by Os. A key point to remember is for a three-box reversal chart, there can never be less than three boxes filled in a column. A second point to remember is that for a price to be plotted, it must be a round number. That is, for a column of rising prices, to advance from, say, 25 to 26, the price must be 26 or higher. There's no rounding up from 25.99. For readers already conversant in point and figure charting, all this is well-known. For readers unfamiliar with the point and figure method, all this may serve to confuse rather than clarify. Thus, an illustration of how to construct a point and figure chart is in order (see Figure 6.1).

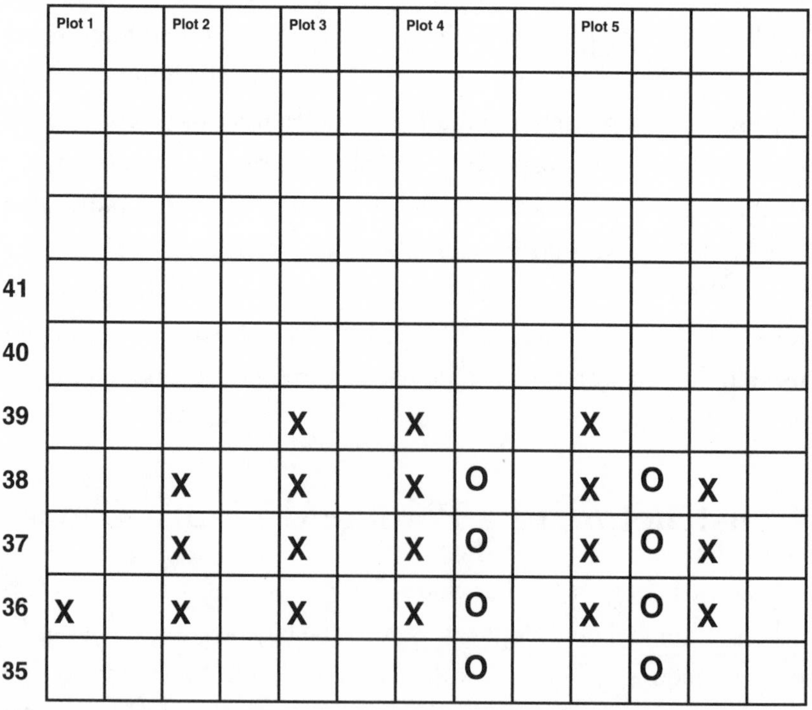

	Plot 1		Plot 2		Plot 3		Plot 4			Plot 5			
41													
40													
39					X		X			X			
38			X		X		X	O		X	O	X	
37			X		X		X	O		X	O	X	
36	X		X		X		X	O		X	O	X	
35								O			O		

Figure 6.1   Constructing a point and figure chart

The stock XYZ in Figure 6.1 shows a series of price changes as follows: 35.5, 36, 36.9, 38.2, 38.8, 39.3, 38, 37.5, 36.3, 35.7, 34.7, 36, 37.2, 38. Each box has a value of one point, and the reversal amount is three boxes. The starting price, at 35.5 is not enough to plot on the graph because a move to 36 or higher is needed. The next price, 36, would be plotted (Plot 1). The next price, at 36.9, would not be plotted because the price must move to or through the next box price (37 in this case). However, the next day, the price moves to 38.2, which means two additional boxes can be filled (37 and 38 in Plot 2). The next price, 38.8, falls short of the next full box price. However, the next number, 39.3 fulfills the requirement of the next full box price and is plotted (Plot 3). This gives us a column of Xs from 36 to 39.

The move to 39 proves to be the high water mark for this rally, as prices turn lower, dropping to 38. Remember, though, this is a three-box reversal chart, so the price must drop a full three points in order to start a column of Os. The price subsequently drops to 37.5 then 36.3. Nothing is yet plotted, though, because the price must drop a full three points from the top price in the column of Xs. This means a drop to 36 or lower is needed. In fact, this is what happens next with the drop to 34.7. So in Plot 4, a column of Os is plotted. Because there was no price at 39 when prices began to drop, the first O is placed at 38 with an additional two Os plotted to complete the drop to 36.

The next day, prices fall further, to 34.7, so an additional O can be plotted at the 35 level. At this point, prices turn higher again, with a move to 36. Although this represents a full-box price, remember, just as a price change of three full boxes was needed to start the column of Os, a rally of three full boxes is needed for a new column of Xs. The stock price continues to rise, moving to 37.2 the next day. Nothing is yet plotted, though, as the price must rise to 38, a level reached the following day. Therefore, a new column of Xs is begun, starting at 36 and rising to 38 (Plot 5). Keep in mind, a column of Xs can only represent rising prices. To mark a move lower, it is necessary to move over one column and begin a new column of Os. With some practice, plotting point and figure charts becomes a relatively simple and quick process. It also allows an investor to update the price movement in a large number of stocks on a daily basis in a short period of time.

Point and Figure Charts as Applied to Major Market Tops and Bottoms: The Horizontal Count

One of the more common uses for point and figure charts is the calculation of anticipated targets for a rally or decline. There are two ways this calculation is determined, the horizontal and the vertical counts. As implied by the name, the horizontal count is determined by the width of a point and figure pattern. This would include a period in which prices move sideways in a relatively narrow range. The width of this range is the basis for the count, which is calculated by multiplying the number of boxes in the count by the box size and then by the reversal amount. In the case of a basing formation, the amount calculated is then typically added to the lowest point of the trading range to establish a target for the ensuing rally. So, for instance, if a trading range, or base, is 10 boxes-wide, with 5 points per box and a three-box reversal method used, the count would be calculated 10 x 5 x 3 = 150. This 150 points would then be added to the value of the lowest box in the range to establish a target price.

A vertical count is usually applied only to the three-box reversal method. It is calculated by counting the number of boxes in a column of Xs or Os. This count is then multiplied by the reversal amount (three for a three-box reversal) to determine the projected target. Wyckoff used only a horizontal count for his calculations; consequently, only this method of establishing a count is used for setting price target ranges on the market tops and bottoms discussed in this chapter.

Although the Wyckoff method has many uses for point and figure charts, for our purposes, their main application is to major market tops and bottoms. The formation of these tops and bottoms is reflected, as just noted, in broad horizontal point and figure patterns. In terms of Wyckoff's Law of Cause and Effect, these horizontal patterns are the cause, and the larger the cause, the larger the likely effect or price target. In other words, the broader the top or bottom formation, the larger the following bull or bear market is likely to be. The extent of the horizontal postings in the topping or bottoming formation is termed the *count*. It is important to note that the count is not a precise tool as an indication of an exact upside or downside target, as will become evident through the examples in this chapter. It is also vital that the count is not done with a target already in mind so that a count is found simply to match expectations. Rather, a count should be done objectively with the target established from the count and not the other way around.

The first step in developing a count in a bottoming pattern is to find a sign of strength. Typically, this is a Last Point of Support (LPS) after a Sign of Strength rally. While there may be several LPSs in a bottoming process, the optimal point to use would be the one defined by the pullback (Backup to the Edge of the Creek) following a Jump Across the Creek, as this normally marks the end of the bottoming process and beginning of the mark up phase of the new bull market. The count is taken from right to left, usually to the first indication the bottoming process has begun, normally the Preliminary Support (PS).

Developing a count for a topping formation is similar. First, identify a rebound following a Sign of Weakness, usually a Last Point of Supply (LPSY). The point to use in this case is typically the top of the rally that serves as a test of the Break Through the Ice, considering this is the point where the topping formation is complete and the markdown phase of the new bear market begins. The count would then be taken from this point across to the left, typically to the Preliminary Supply (PSY) as the first indication a topping process has begun. This might seem like a lot of points to consider. But the simple way to remember them is to use the last and first signs of weakness in a topping pattern and the last and first signs of strength in a bottoming pattern. Plus these points would already have been identified when doing the initial Wyckoff analysis of the market tops and bottoms.

The count itself is established simply by counting the number of boxes from the starting to the ending points. In the case of a market bottom, that would be the number of boxes between the LPS and Preliminary Support. It is important to remember that all boxes, including empty boxes, are included in the count. The projected range is then established by multiplying the number of boxes in the count by the point value for each box and by the reversal amount. Thus, a 3-box reversal point and figure graph with box sizes of 10 points each and a horizontal count of 15 would have a projected count of 450 points: 10 x 15 x 3 = 450.

With the count established, the next step is to determine the target. However, rather than identifying a specific price target, the Wyckoff method establishes a target range. The initial point used to establish a target range is the level at which the count itself was taken. For example, in a bottoming pattern, the level of the count would be established by the Last Point of Support (LPS). The target price is identified by adding the count to the level of that Last Point of Support. Thus a horizontal count of 300 taken from a LPS at a level at 775 would suggest a target price of 1075.

The target range is then established by adding the count to the lowest point in the basing pattern, often a Spring, test of a Spring, Shakeout, or Selling Climax. It is usually best to use the most conservative count when establishing a range. Typically, this means using the Sign of Strength that represents the lowest price in the bottoming formation. Thus if a Spring were to drop to a level below that of the Selling Climax, the Spring would be used to establish the range.

Taking the previous example, if the Spring were at a level of 700, then the target range would be 1000 (Spring price: 700 + 300 = 1000) to 1075 (Last Point of Support price: 775 + 300 = 1075).

A similar process is used in establishing a range from a topping formation. First, establish the count. Most often, the count begins at the level of a sign of weakness, usually the Last Point of Supply. When this point is identified, count the boxes from right to left to the first indication the topping process has begun, usually the point of Preliminary Supply. The next step is to subtract the count from the level where the count started, which again, is typically the LPSY. The target range is then established by subtracting the count from the highest point of a topping pattern such as a Buying Climax or Upthrust. So in the case of a top where the Upthrust represents the highest price, the target range would be determined by subtracting the count from the highest price in the Upthrust and also from the price of the LPSY.

To re-emphasize an earlier point before we get to the illustrations: counts are to be used only as an indication of possible targets. They should never be considered as indicating exact levels. The count provides no indication of whether the bull or bear market will reach or overshoot the target range. In general, we have found using price targets to be more hazardous to investment success than not. For instance, say a rally begins to falter well below its target. The temptation might be to ignore warning signs of a possible significant downside reversal. After all, the target has not yet been reached! Or a rally may overshoot its target, raising the temptation to sell, only to see prices continue to move substantially higher. In all cases, the measures already detailed in identifying a market top or bottom should predominate over any price target range. The utility of the target range is solely in its role as a possible confirming element of other, more reliable, indications of a top or bottom formation. With that caveat, let's look at how the Law of Cause and Effect can be applied to the market tops and bottoms discussed in previous chapters.

The 1969 Market Top and Targets for the Bear Market

Taking the major tops and bottoms already discussed in chronological order, our initial venture into establishing a count is with the market top in 1968–1969 (Figure 6.2). The first step is to establish the level at which to take the count. In this case, this is the Last Point of Supply (LPSY). We then count from right to left to the initial sign of weakness, the point of Preliminary Supply (PSY). Keep in mind, not all the columns will necessarily be filled with an X or an O, but all must be counted nonetheless. Moving right to left from the LPSY to PSY establishes a total of 11 boxes. Given the relatively low price of the DJIA in 1969, we have assigned a box size of 10 points per box. Because this is a three-box reversal chart, the projected range is calculated by multiplying the box size (10) by the horizontal count (11) and the box size (3). So 10 x 11 x 3 = 330 points.

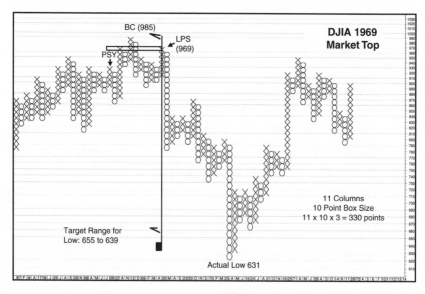

Charts created with Metastock, a Thomson Reuters product.

Figure 6.2   Establishing a count at the 1969 market top

With the projected count calculated, the next step is to determine the target range to the downside. The initial measuring point is typically the place where the count begins, in this case at the Last Point of Supply. The DJIA close at this point was at 969. The downside projection, though, should be as conservative as possible, meaning another measurement should be taken from the highest level of the topping process. In this case, the highest point was set on November 29, 1968, when the DJIA reached a level of 985. Note that rather than forming a top in a Buying Climax, the peak in the bull market was marked by about a week of churning action. Churning is a process in which prices fail to show any significant upside progress despite heavy volume. As such, it usually marks a period of distribution, as enough Supply is coming on the market to overcome the existing Demand. Although less dramatic than a Buying Climax, this churning action, when it occurs at the top of a substantial rally, can be just as decisive in marking a significant market top.

The downside projection for the bear market can now be calculated by subtracting the count from the two measuring points, the peak of these few days of churning (at 985) and LPSY (at 969). This produces a downside target range of 655 to 639 (985 - 330 = 655; 969 - 330 = 639). The actual close for the DJIA at the bear market low was on May 26, 1970, with a close at 631.16 and intraday low at 627.46. Keep in mind, and as will become apparent in subsequent examples, not all projections, either to the upside or downside, are as precise as this initial study. It is vital to remember these projections serve only as guides, not as hard and fast targets. Investors should always defer to market conditions themselves in determining whether a bull or bear market has concluded, regardless of whether or not a projected target has been reached.

One final note on chart construction—beginning in the early 1990s, data providers began supplying the actual high and low for the DJIA. Prior to that, the standard was the theoretical high and low (based on a calculation that all 30 DJIA stocks made their highs and lows for the session simultaneously). Consequently, highs and lows cited in the charts from the 60s, 70s, and 80s are based on the theoretical calculation. DJIA highs and lows from 2000 forward are cited using the actual high and low for a given day. This may seem like a rather esoteric and largely irrelevant difference. However, we found using the theoretical versus actual daily highs and lows in the DJIA did make a clear difference in the projected target ranges, with the actual high and low producing a more accurate target.

The 1970 Market Bottom and Targets for the 1970–1973 Bull Market

Our next study (Figure 6.3) is the 1970 market bottom and subsequent bull market to the 1973 top. The first step is to establish the level where the count should be taken. For a market bottom, the pullback following a Sign of Strength rally is the recommended starting point for a count. This is typically the Last Point of Support (LPS). In the 1970 bottom, the applicable Sign of Strength rally is the one that followed the Jump Across the Creek. The final Last Point of Support (LPS, at 707) marked the beginning of the strong initial rally in the 1970–1973 bull market. The count is then made from right to left to the first indication the bear market was concluding. For a market bottom, this first point is normally Preliminary Support (PS). Moving from right to left from the LPS to PS results in a count of 10 boxes (columns). Remember, a column does not have to be filled to be included in the count. Because the rally to the 1973 high took the DJIA over 1000, we used a box size of 11 points, slightly larger than the 10 points used for the 1969 top. And given this is also a three-box reversal chart, the calculation for the projected range is 10 (number of columns) x 11 (box size) x 3 (reversal amount) = 330 point range.

When the count is established, the next step is to choose the levels used for determining the target range. A conservative projection uses the low point of the bottoming process which, for the 1970 bottom, was the Selling Climax at a DJIA level of 631. The second level is where the count began, at the LPS at 707. Adding the 330 projected range to the SC low and to the LPS produces a target range of 961 to 1037. In this case, both fell short of the actual high of 1051, set on January 11, 1973. The projected high for the bull market, however, was probably close enough to alert an investor to begin looking for signs of a market top—signs that, as it turned out, were quick to develop.

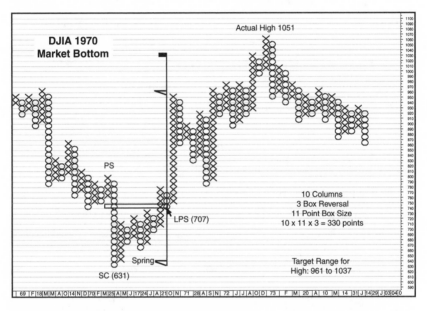

Charts created with Metastock, a Thomson Reuters product.

Figure 6.3   Establishing a count at the 1970 market bottom

The 1972–73 Market Top and the Severe Bear Market into the 1975 Low

The 1972–1973 top (Figure 6.4) offers an object lesson about placing too much emphasis on a projected range. Although the 1973–1974 bear market was the most severe since the 1930s, the topping pattern at the end of the 1970–1972 bull market was compact and provided little evidence of the carnage to come. Other interpretations of the top might produce a different, more extensive count. However, the levels we have used appear to conform most closely to both a traditional Wyckoff analysis and to the actions of Lowry's Buying Power and

Selling Pressure Indexes. Accordingly, we identified the Last Point of Supply at the test of the Ice in mid-February at a level of 997. Counting right to left to Preliminary Supply yielded a count of just 5 boxes. We used an 11-point box size, consistent with the chart for the 1970 market bottom. This produced a projected count of 165 (11 x 3 x 5). Subtracting this count from the highest level of the topping formation, in this case the Buying Climax at 1051, and from the LPSY at 997 produced a target range of 886 to 832. As it turned out, this range was well short of the eventual bottom at 577, set in December 1974. The range, however, did identify the prolonged distribution pattern December 1973 to June 1974, which preceded the plunge to the final low of the bear market. Apart from unabashed curve fitting, any logical count from this December to June trading range carries far below the market's actual low, providing no useful guide as to the extent of the decline when prices broke down from the range. Accordingly, the 1972–73 market top has to be noted as a cautionary example of the risk entailed in overemphasizing targets as part of an analysis.

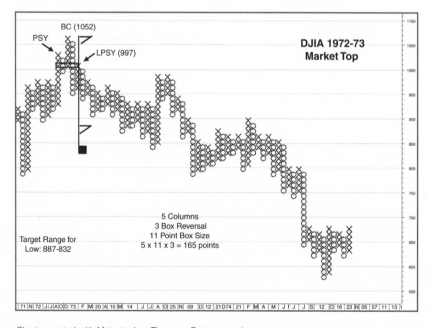

Charts created with Metastock, a Thomson Reuters product.

Figure 6.4   Establishing a count at the 1972–73 market top

The 1974–1975 Market Bottom

The market bottom in 1974–1975 (see Figure 6.5) ended first with an initial Spring and then with another Spring in December, as prices dropped to a marginal new low but on rising Demand and falling Supply. The rally that followed the Spring represented a Sign of Strength, so our count begins on the pullback from this rally to the Last Point of Support.

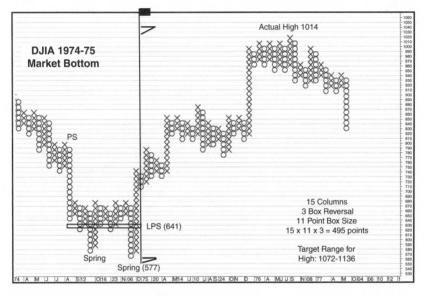

Charts created with Metastock, a Thomson Reuters product.

Figure 6.5   Establishing a count at the 1974–75 market bottom

The limitations of using a three-box reversal chart are evident in this count, as the appropriate LPS came on a pullback in price too small to show up on the chart. Therefore, our count begins with the column representing the Sign of Strength rally off the Spring low. The count is taken right to left to the initial sign of a bottoming process, the Preliminary Support, encompassing 15 boxes. This produced a count of 495 (15 x 11 x 3 = 495). The most conservative target uses the close from the low of the trading range, which, in this case is the low formed by the Spring in December 1974, at 577. The other boundary for the target range for a market top is then established by adding the count to the level of the LPS at 641. The result is a target range of 1072 to 1136. As it turned out, this range was a little overoptimistic, as the actual high for the 1975–1976 bull market was set on September 21–22, 1976, at a close of 1014 and an intraday high at 1026. Both the close and intraday high were below the target range but were close enough nonetheless to alert an investor that the topping activity associated with the sideways movement beginning in early 1976 could be part of a major top.

The Drawn-Out Market Top in 1976

The market top in 1976 (Figure 6.6) was a long, drawn out affair encompassing most of the year. In fact, it is possible to extend the topping process to the recovery high reached in late December. This last gasp rally, however, is probably best treated as a secondary topping pattern apart from the major top formed between February and September. Even excluding the rally to the December high as part of the topping process, our count results in a target range considerably below the actual market low in March 1980.

Counts at market tops begin with the rebound following a clear sign of weakness. In this case, the Sign of Weakness (SOW) followed the Upthrust to a new rally high in late September. This rapid decline was followed by a weak rebound to the Last Point of Supply in late October/early November. Our count, therefore starts at this LPSY and moves to the left to the first sign of a possible major top at the point of Preliminary Supply for a total of 11 boxes. Multiplying the 11 boxes by the box size of 11 and the 3-point reversal amount produces a count of 363. To establish the target range for a market bottom, we use the closing prices at the LPSY at 966 and at the Upthrust at 1014. Subtracting the 363 count from these two levels results in a target range of 651 to 603. This range proved too ambitious, as the actual market low was set in a classic selling climax on "Silver Thursday" March 27, 1980, the day the Hunt silver bubble burst. The intraday low, at 730 and closing low at 760, are both well above the target range. This, then, provides another good example of not allowing a projected target to obscure signs of an important market bottom.

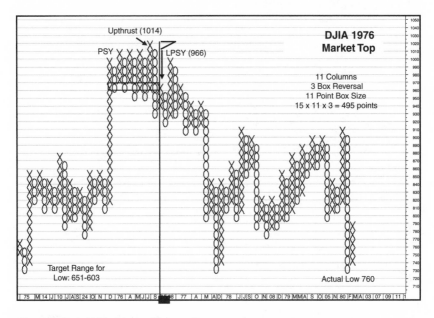

Charts created with Metastock, a Thomson Reuters product.

Figure 6.6   Establishing a count at the 1976 market top

The 1981 Market Top and Approaching End of the Secular Bear Market

The bull market initiated by the selling climax on "Silver Thursday" in March 1980 proved short-lived, as the topping process began with a point of Preliminary Supply in November 1980 (Figure 6.7). The subsequent bear market, which lasted until August 1982, proved to be the last gasp of the secular bear that had begun in 1966. This bear market also marked a sea change for market leadership, as the inflation-sensitive energy, precious metals, and basic materials stocks that had thrived in the late 1970s took a back seat to stocks that bene-fited from then-Federal Reserve Chairman Paul Volcker's successful slaying of inflation. Thus, market leadership for much of the new sec-ular bull market passed to financial, consumer staples, utility, and eventually to technology stocks in the bubble that ushered in the start of a new secular bear market in 2000.

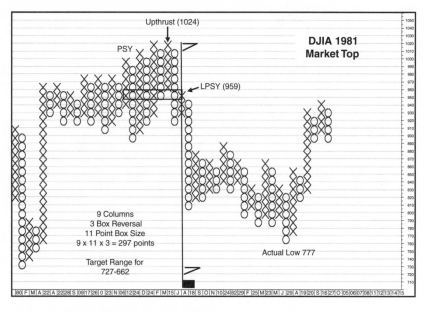

Charts created with Metastock, a Thomson Reuters product.

Figure 6.7   Establishing a count at the 1981 market top

The initial point for a count begins with the rebound to the LPSY following the sharp decline and Sign of Weakness from the Upthrust to 1024. Counting right to left to the column representing the point of PSY encompasses 9 boxes. The box size for this chart is 11 points. As this is also a three-box reversal chart, the count would be calculated as 9 x 11 x 3 = 297 points. The target range for the bottom of the bear market is established by subtracting 297 from the level of the LPSY at 959 and from the top of the Upthrust at 1024. This produces a target range of 727 to 662. As has been the case with most of the projections from market tops, this range proved too pessimistic, given the actual closing low, on August 11, 1982, was at 777, with an intraday low set on April 6 at 770. Once again, though, the primary target of 727 was close enough to alert an investor a bottoming process that began in the low-800s/high-700s had the potential for a major market low.

The 1982 Market Bottom and the Start of the Secular Bull Market 1982–2000

One of the best indications the market bottom in 1982 (Figure 6.8) represented more than another cyclical low in an ongoing secular bear market was the extremely heavy volume that followed the August 11, 1982, market bottom. The sea change in leadership, from stocks that benefited from rising inflation to those most likely to benefit from falling inflation or disinflation provided another indication a major trend change for the stock market could be underway.

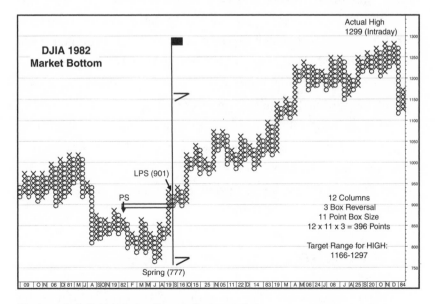

Charts created with Metastock, a Thomson Reuters product.

Figure 6.8   Establishing a count at the 1982 market bottom

The beginning of the end of the secular bear market began quietly enough with a point of Preliminary Support that included a 90%

Up Day. After a Selling Climax and several secondary tests of support, the final stage of the bottoming process began with a Spring and Sign of Strength rally that broke out to a new recovery high. This rally was followed by a minor pullback that created the starting point for our count, the Last Point of Support. In this case, given that the LPS occurred above the top of the bottoming process, the level of the count appears odd, as it includes no filled boxes.

As pointed out earlier, though, all boxes, whether filled or not, are included in the count. Starting at the LPS and moving to the left, we count 12 boxes (or columns in this case). The box size for this chart remains at 11 points per box, and the reversal amount remains at 3 boxes. Thus the count is calculated 12 x 11 x 3 = 396 points. The levels used to establish a target range are at the low point of the market bottom, at the Spring with a closing level at 777, and at the LPS, with a closing level at 901. Adding the count to these two levels results in a target range between 1166 and 1297. This is one instance where the count produced a range that, for all intents and purposes, called the market top. The closing high for the bull market was set on January 6, 1984, at 1287, with an intraday high set on January 13 at 1299, just two points above the upper end of the target range at 1297. But, as is evident in previous examples, projections this close are more the exception than the rule. It is therefore vital to remember that these projected targets for both bull and bear markets should be treated as guidelines rather than as levels set in stone, with the action of the market itself providing the best evidence whether or not a major top or bottom is in the process of forming.

The 2002–2003 Market Bottom

At this point, we are skipping to the 2003 market bottom as the unusual characteristics of the 2000 market top are such that it deserves a chapter all by itself.

The first indication that the 2000–2003 bear market (Figure 6.9) was coming to an end was a rally on heavy volume and a 90% Up Day in early July 2002. This was followed later in the month with a classic Selling Climax that was subsequently tested by a shakeout in October and Spring in March 2003. This Spring was followed by a Sign of Strength rally that included another 90% Up Day and also entailed a breakout (Jump Across the Creek in Wyckoff terms). The subsequent pullback to test the breakout was the LPS in the bottoming pattern and serves as the starting point for our count.

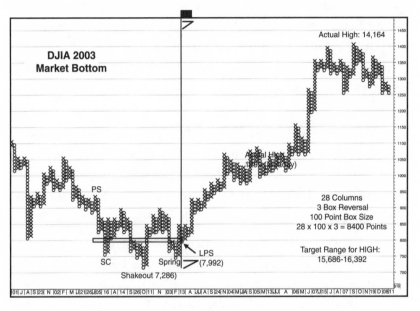

Charts created with Metastock, a Thomson Reuters product.

Figure 6.9   Establishing a count at the 2002–2003 market bottom

Moving right to left to the point of Preliminary Support yields a count of 28 boxes. Because the DJIA has moved into five-digit territory, the size of the boxes used in the point and figure chart has increased dramatically to 100 points per box. The three-box reversal method remains the same. The calculation for the count is therefore 100 x 28 x 3 = 8400 points. The target range is established by adding the count to the low point of the bottoming pattern—in this case at the October 2002 Shakeout, with a DJIA close at 7286, and at the level of the LPS, at a close of 7992. Given the count of 8400, this

yields a target range of 15,686 to 16,392. This projection was well off
the mark, as the final high of the 2003–2007 bull market was on October 9 2007, at 14,164, with an intraday high set on October 11 at
14,198. There is no way to rationalize this target as providing any
guidance in the formation of the 2007 market peak, which began the
topping process about 1600 points below the minimum target.

The 2002–2003 market bottom is one instance, however, that
readily lends itself to an alternative count. In this alternative, the
count is based on an apparent "head and shoulders" formation, with
the July 2002 Selling Climax serving as the left shoulder, the October
Shakeout at the head, and the March 2003 Spring as the right shoulder. Beginning at the right shoulder and concluding at the left shoulder results in a count of 23 boxes. Using the same 100-point box size
and three-box reversal method yields a projected range of 6900.
Adding this range of 6900 to the closing low of the 2002–2003 market
bottom of 7287 on October 9, 2002, produces a target of 14187. With
an actual closing high at 14,164 and intraday high at 14,198, this alternative count yields a result that virtually matches the actual high.

We should point out, though, that attempting to find alternative
counts can end up causing more confusion than clarification, especially if an alternative count varies widely, as this one does, from the
traditional count. Therefore, our recommendation is to stick with the
traditional count, using the initial and final points of weakness (Preliminary Supply and Last Point of Supply) as the boundaries for a
count at a market top and the initial and final signs of strength (Preliminary Support and Last Point of Support) for market bottoms.

The 2007 Market Top and Start
of the Worst Bear Market Since
the 1929–32 Wipeout

The preamble to the worst bear market since 1929–1932 started
out with a heavy volume decline from a new bull market high in

mid-July, marking a point of Preliminary Supply (Figure 6.10). The final top, in mid-October, was a relatively quiet affair, on light volume with no evidence of the panic buying that sometimes accompanies a market peak. However, prices moved steadily lower from there, eventually breaking down in early January 2008 in a crescendo of selling. The rebound from this panic selling comprised a test of the breakdown level—in Wyckoff terms, testing the Break through the Ice—and also a LPSY, providing the start for our point and figure count.

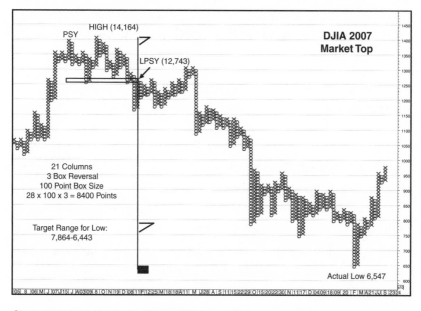

Charts created with Metastock, a Thomson Reuters product.

Figure 6.10   Establishing a count at the 2007 market top

As has been the case with other market tops or bottoms, there are relatively few filled boxes in the count starting with the LPSY and carrying over to the point of PSY. However, it is the number of columns that is important, not whether the columns include filled boxes. Moving from right to left on the chart results in a horizontal count of 21 boxes. As was done with the 2002–2003 market bottom, a box size of 100 points is used for the DJIA. Taking the count of 21 boxes times the box size and the three-box reversal method results in 21 x 100 x 3 = 6300. One boundary of the target range for the bear market is calculated by subtracting 6300 from the LPSY, at a closing price of 12,743, producing a downside target of 6443. The other boundary of the target range, again using the most conservative measurement, which means using the high point of the topping pattern, is then calculated from the October market peak, with a close at 14,164. This produces a target range from 7864 to 6443. The actual closing low for the bear market, on March 9, 2009, was at 6547, about 100 points above the bottom of our projected range—not bad for a decline that took the DJIA down by over 7600 points, or nearly 54%.

Conclusion

This chapter began with a point and figure count that almost exactly targeted the actual bottom for a bear market and ended the chapter the same way. In between though, there were several examples of targets that were either far short or well above the actual extent of the bear and bull markets they purported to measure. Therefore, it is key to remember targets based on these horizontal counts are meant only as guidelines. Every once in a while the count might seem magical in pinpointing the actual high or low for a bull or bear market. But in the final analysis, the Wyckoff rules of price and volume, assisted by measures of Supply and Demand, such as Lowry's Buying Power and Selling Pressure Indexes, are much more accurate in identifying the starting and ending points of major market tops and bottoms.

Endnote

[1] Charles D. Kirkpatrick and Julie R Dahlquist, *Technical Analysis: The Complete Resource for Financial Market Technicians* (Upper Saddle River, N.J.: FT Press, 2006).

7

Identifying Major Market Tops and Bottoms: Other Tools to Consider

A basic tenet of virtually any analytical technique is the more evidence that points to a conclusion, the more likely that conclusion will be valid. In general terms, this is called the weight of evidence and applies equally to an examination of market conditions.

Thus far, we have discussed using the Wyckoff laws of Supply and Demand and Effort vs. Result in helping identify market tops and bottoms, together with Lowry's application of the Law of Supply and Demand through the Buying Power and Selling Pressure Indexes. We have also discussed Wyckoff's Law of Cause and Effect as used in establishing price targets for bull and bear markets through horizontal counts on point and figure charts. In terms of weight of evidence, therefore, we have price/volume action and independent measures of Buying and Selling, plus rough guidelines as to the likely extent of a bull or bear market. In this chapter, we add to this weight of evidence by introducing two other tools that have proved useful over the years in identifying major market tops and bottoms.

The NYSE Advance–Decline

Our first additional tool is an Advance–Decline Line based on issues traded on the New York Stock Exchange. Historically, the NYSE Advance–Decline Line has served as a sort of "canary in the coal mine" in providing a forewarning of major market tops. As an indicator, the Advance–Decline Line first came into use in the 1920s and 1930s through the work of Leonard P. Ayers, contemporaneous with the work of Wyckoff and Lowry. In its simplest terms, an Advance–Decline Line (or A–D Line as it is frequently abbreviated), is a cumulative net total of the issues advancing and declining on a day-to-day basis on an Exchange (the NYSE, for example) or in a market index such as the S&P 500. Thus, if there were 2520 issues advancing on the NYSE today and 488 declining, a net of 2032 would be added to the cumulative total. In contrast, if today had more declining than advancing issues, the net amount would be subtracted from the cumulative total. The result is a line that normally rises during a bull market and falls during a bear market. The utility of the A–D Line occurs when it fails to confirm new rally highs in a bull market.

This simple method of calculating an A–D Line is the most common, but there are other methods in use as well. One of the more popular is a "normalized" A–D Line. This normalization applies largely to the NYSE A–D Line and is intended to adjust for the larger number of issues traded today than were traded 30 or 40 years ago. The A–D Line is normalized by dividing the net amount of advancing and declining issues by the total number of issues traded that day (including those that are unchanged). The result is then added to the cumulative total just as in the regular A–D Line. For example, there were 1500 advancing issues today and 1300 declining issues with a total of 3140 issues traded (the total includes unchanged issues). Subtracting the 1300 declining issues from 1500 advancing issues yields a net of 200 issues. This net amount is then divided by the total number of issues traded, 3140, yielding a normalized number of .064. This amount is then added (given there are more advancing than declining issues today) to our cumulative total to produce the updated A–D Line. More declining issues would produce a negative number, which would be added to the cumulative total, resulting in a drop in the A–D Line for the day. We have plotted both the regular NYSE A–D

Line and its normalized equivalent and found no major differences between the two, especially when applied to identifying major market tops and bottoms. Therefore, all the illustrations in this chapter use the simple version of the NYSE A–D Line.

Advance–Decline Lines and Major Market Tops and Bottoms

The role played by A–D Lines, most often the Composite NYSE A–D Line, in identifying market tops is as a nonconfirming indicator. We introduced the concept of negative divergences in discussing the Buying Power and Selling Pressure indexes as confirming or failing to confirm price highs and lows during the formation of major market tops and bottoms. The Composite NYSE A–D Line plays a similar role in failing to confirm, or negatively diverging from, rally highs in price. To use a recent example, Figure 7.1 shows the S&P 500 Index during the formation of the 2007 market top. The bottom plot on the graph is the Composite (also called the all-issues) NYSE A–D Line.[1] Note that both the price of the S&P Index and the A–D Line made new rally highs in early June 2007. After about a month of trading sideways, the S&P 500 renewed its rally, recording another new high in mid-July. Notice, however, the July peak in the A–D Line is below its level in early June—that is, the A–D Line has failed to confirm the price high, setting up a negative divergence. This divergence then continues with the level of the A–D Line far below both its June or July readings at the nominal new rally high set by the S&P 500 Index in mid-October.

One reason for the development of this negative divergence between the price indexes and the A–D Line is, as a bull market progresses, buying typically becomes more selective. This selectivity can be a result of investors viewing some stocks as overextended in their rallies or others as fundamentally overvalued. However, that's only part of the story. Although the exact number varies slightly according to the source, approximately 50% of the issues traded on the NYSE are what might be classified as non-operating company issues. That is, they are something other than common stocks. These non-operating company issues include closed-end bond funds, preferred stocks, and American Depository Receipts (ADR) of foreign stocks. Notice that with the exception of the ADRs, these non-operating company issues tend to be sensitive to interest rates and therefore can act more as bond surrogates than common stocks.

Charts created with Metastock, a Thomson Reuters product.

Figure 7.1   The NYSE A–D Line at the 2007 market top

These interest-sensitive issues thus can play a role in the development of A–D Line negative divergences along with the other reasons for increasingly selective buying. As has been discussed in works by Martin Pring and John Murphy, among others, interest rate cycles tend to lead cycles in the equity market. That is, interest rates typically begin to rise as a business cycle matures. Figure 7.2 plots the yield on the 10-year treasury note versus the S&P 500. As is evident from the graph, interest rates begin rising prior to the major tops in the stock market—sometimes well in advance. Although these non-operating company issues can be carried along higher with the prevailing bullish sentiment, eventually, the lagging prices of these issues, due to higher interest rates, causes more and more selling, thus contributing to an increase in declining issues even as the equity market continues to climb. In fact, some studies have shown an A–D Line composed entirely of these interest-sensitive issues can provide an even earlier warning of a market top than the Composite A–D Line.

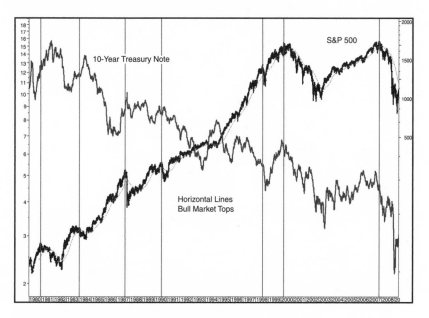

Charts created with Metastock, a Thomson Reuters product.

Figure 7.2   The 10-year treasury note typically leads trend changes in the S&P 500

Historically, divergences between the Composite NY A–D Line and the major market indexes have been one of the most reliable indications of the approaching end of a bull market. As shown in Table 7.1, of the 16 bull market tops since 1940, there have been only three instances, in 1946, 1952, and 1976, when no negative divergence occurred prior to the market top. However, lead times can vary widely, from an extreme of 23 months prior to the 2000 market top to

just 1 month prior to the 1956 peak. On average, though, the lead
time has been around 10 months and about 7½ months ex the outlier
years in 1973 and 2000.

**TABLE 7.1   NYSE All-Issues Advance-Decline Line Divergences at Bull
Market Tops**

Date of Bull Mkt Top	Divergence? Yes/No	Period Between Divergence and Top
May 1946	No	No divergence
Dec 1952	No	No divergence
Apr 1956	Yes	1 month
Jan 1960	Yes	10 month
Dec 1961	Yes	7 month
Feb 1966	Yes	10 month
Dec 1968	Yes	17 month
Jan 1973	Yes	21 month
Sept 1976	No	No divergence
Apr 1981	Yes	7 month
Jan 1984	Yes	7 month
Aug 1987	Yes	5 month
Jul 1990	Yes	11 month
Jul 1998	Yes	3 month
Mar 2000	Yes	23 month
Oct 2007	Yes	4 month
		Avg: 9.7 months
		Avg Ex '73/'00: 7.5 mos
		Median: 7 months

In both 1973 and 2000, the much larger lag between the peak in
the A–D Line and the market top appeared due to two factors. The
bull market that peaked in 1973 was narrowly based and driven by the
so-called "Nifty-Fifty" stocks, just as the bull market to the 2000 peak
was fueled by the dot-com bubble. Also, leading up to both the 1973
and 2000 market tops, small- and mid-cap stocks were in the midst of
a period of cyclical underperformance to the big-cap stocks. Together,
these two factors were unique to these two market tops and account

for much of the unusually long lead time between the A–D Line and the market peaks. In contrast, the lack of a negative divergence at the 1976 market top appeared due to an up cycle in relative performance by mid- and small-caps that followed the down cycle prior to the 1973 market top. In fact, reflecting the rally by small- and mid-caps, the A–D Line continued to climb after the DJIA peaked in September 1976, moving steadily higher throughout the plunge in the DJIA to the February 1977 low and not peaking until early September 1977.

Figures 7.3–7.7 show the NYSE all-issues A–D Line at the major market tops in 1969, 1973, 1976, 1981, and 2000. Although we have not included graphs for the 1984, 1987, 1991, or 1998 market tops, negative divergences between the A–D Line and the market indexes are not exclusive to secular bear markets such as the one from 1966 to 1982. They apply just as well to those four market tops in the secular bull market that lasted from 1982 to 2000.

Charts created with Metastock, a Thomson Reuters product.

Figure 7.3   NYSE A_D Line divergence at the 1968 market top

The negative divergence at the December 1968 market peak (Figure 7.3) is very minor but did exist, suggesting buying had become more selective in the rally to the 1969 peak than in the advance to the prior high in the bull market, in September, 1967. At 17 months, this lag between the peak in the A–D Line and market peak is the third longest, after the 1973 and 2000 market tops. Figure 7.4 shows the steady deterioration in market breadth[3] prior to the 1973 market high. As explained earlier, much of this deterioration was due to the investment theme du jour, the so-called Nifty-Fifty or one-decision (buy it and forget it) stocks, which caused buying to be focused on a very select number of mostly big-cap issues.

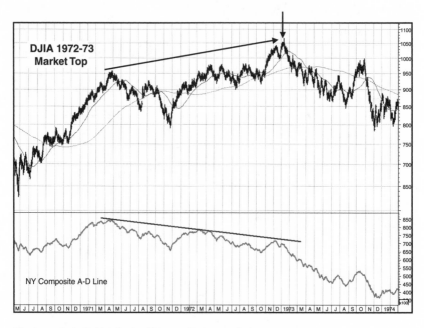

Charts created with Metastock, a Thomson Reuters product.

Figure 7.4   NYSE A–D Line at the 1972-73 market top

The one failure of the A–D Line to forecast a market top in our study occurred in 1976. As shown in Figure 7.5, the A–D remained in an uptrend dating back to the 1975 market low throughout the topping formation in 1976. In fact, as mentioned earlier, the NYSE A–D

Line remained in an uptrend, not only throughout the topping forma-tion, but also through the first two years of the 1976–80 bear market. While the 1973–74 bear market discredited the Nifty-Fifty stocks, virtually all of which cratered during the market decline, small- and mid-cap stocks, which had lagged going into the 1973 market top, enjoyed somewhat of a renaissance. Because small- and mid-caps far outnumber big caps on the NYSE, strength in these issues resulted in a rising A–D Line while the market indexes were falling.

Charts created with Metastock, a Thomson Reuters product.

Figure 7.5   No divergence by the NYSE A–D Line at the 1976 market top

As shown in Figure 7.6, the A–D Line divergence prior to the 1981 market high began in September 1980, matching the average and median lag time of seven months. The biggest lag between the peak in the A–D Line and the market indexes in the years we have covered occurred prior to the 2000 market top (Figure 7.7). In this case, the high in the A–D Line occurred in April, 1998, which actually preceded the July–October 1998 minor bear market. However, rather than rebounding after that bear market had run its course, the A–D

Line continued its descent, finally bottoming just about the time the market indexes peaked in early 2000. As discussed earlier, much of this lag in the A–D figures was due to a cyclical downturn by small- and mid-cap stocks. Ironically, for much of the 2000–2003 bear market, while big-cap and especially big-cap technology stocks, were being decimated, small- and mid-caps prospered. In fact, both the S&P Mid and Small Cap indexes continued to rally throughout the first couple years of the 2000–2003 bear market, reaching new rally highs in April, 2002. We discuss this further in Chapter 8, "The Curious Case of the 2000–2001 Market Top and Demise of the Secular Bull Market," which is devoted to the unique aspects of the 2000–2001 market top.

Charts created with Metastock, a Thomson Reuters product.

Figure 7.6   NSYE A–D Line at the 1981 market top

From these examples, it seems clear the A–D Line has historically provided regular warnings of impending market tops. It could be argued, of course, a lead time of 17 or 23 months seems of little use in timing a market top. In both cases, though, it is the environment of selective buying, combined with the other tools of price/volume, Supply/Demand, and target ranges that provide the evidence an important trend change is occurring.

Charts created with Metastock, a Thomson Reuters product.

Figure 7.7   The long decline in the NYSE A–D Line prior to the 2000 market top

At this point, a logical question is, while we have pointed out the utility of A–D Lines in anticipating market tops, what about market bottoms? In fact, in our coverage of market tops and bottoms since 1940, there are no instances when the NYSE A–D Line provided any help in identifying a major market bottom. To the contrary, in every major market bottom since 1940, the NYSE A–D Line recorded a new low right along with the price indexes. For a divergence to develop at a market bottom, there needs to be a pattern of increasingly selective selling. This selective selling results in a rising A–D line, which fails to confirm the lowest levels reached by the major price indexes in the bear market. That is, although the market indexes record a new low, the A–D Line is, at that point, above its most recent low, thus forming a positive (rather than negative) divergence with the market indexes.

However, history shows no such positive divergence at any bear market bottom in at least the past 70 years. And there appears to be a logical reason for a lack of A–D Line divergences at market bottoms. At market tops, selling is typically more fragmented, as there are any number of investors who are yet to be convinced the market has reached an important top. Therefore, selective, rather than wide-spread, selling continues throughout much of the formation of a market top. In contrast, a market bottom is often marked by panic selling in a climax where there is a wholesale dumping of stock. Put more directly, not everyone sells at once at a market top, but they tend to sell en mass at a market bottom. Thus, at market bottoms, there is little opportunity for the selectivity that allows for the A–D Line divergences at market tops.

Operating Companies Only Advance–Decline Lines

In recent years, concerns have developed that movements in the equity market are decoupling from long-term interest rates. This, in turn, calls into question the reliability of the all-issues A–D Line as a forecasting tool. Although the examples already discussed appear to discount this possibility, the use of a common stock-only A–D Line has become more popular. Simply put, an *operating companies only* (OCO) A–D Line excludes all non-common stock issues traded on the NYSE. The NYSE publishes breadth figures using common stocks only, and these data are most readily available on a weekly basis in *Barrons.* Consequently, construction of a common stock-only A–D Line requires no access to special data. However, as Charles Kirk-patrick points out in his book *Technical Analysis: The Complete*

Resource for Financial Market Technicians,[2] beginning in 2005, the NYSE changed its reporting requirements for common stocks, including only those issues with three or fewer letters in their ticker symbols. Consequently, the statistics before 2005 are not directly compatible with those that came after that date. There are, however, services, such as Carl Swenlin's "Decision Point," that calculate their own operating companies only data that avoid this lack of compatibility. But as is pointed out later in this chapter, a long history is not needed to construct an OCO A–D Line useful for warning of market tops.

Comparisons between the NY all-issues A–D Line and its OCO counterpart are often helpful in identifying periods when gains in the A–D Line are due more to strength in the bond market than equity market. Typically, in those instances, the all-issues A–D Line will be climbing at a greater pace than the OCO Line. In these cases, the concern is a bond market rally could be masking greater weakness in the equity market. Thus far, though, disparities in performance between the two A–D Lines have been minimal at major market tops. Figure 7.8 shows a comparison of the NY Composite (all-issues) A–D Line and the OCO A–D Line at the 2007 market top. As can be seen, both A–D Lines failed to confirm the higher high set by the S&P 500 in July 2007, establishing a negative divergence and warning that a major top could be forming. Both A–D Lines were then well below their July levels when the S&P 500 set another new rally high in October 2007, further emphasizing the lack of breadth behind the rally. As can also be seen, a 120-day simple moving average can be helpful in identifying changes in trend for the OCO A–D Line.

Unfortunately, the OCO A–D Line was of no more help than the all-issues A–D in the rally to the 2000 market top, as both peaked in April 1998 and were in strong downtrends at the time of the early 2000 market highs. Judging by the history of market tops since 1992 (which is as far back as Lowry's data go), there appears to be no compelling reason to keep an OCO A–D Line, given that it has thus far moved in accord with the all-issues A–D Line in establishing divergences prior to the three major market tops—1998, 2000, and 2007—since the early 1990s. That said, given the ease with which an OCO A–D Line can be constructed and maintained in today's technology age, there seems little reason not to keep both—just in case.

Charts created with Metastock, a Thomson Reuters product.

Figure 7.8   The NYSE all-issues A–D Line and NY OCO A–D Line at the 2007 market top

The Cyclical Nature of Advance–Decline Lines

Before moving on to our next tool for identifying major market tops, there is one final but important point to make about using A–D Lines. Up until early 2005, the NY Composite A–D Line had a general downward bias in that it had never exceeded its 1957 peak reading (Figure 7.9). This caused some analysts to downplay the use of the A–D Line in identifying market tops because it was always (at least until 2005) below its peak reading. As such, it could not be considered as negatively diverging from a price index making new all-time highs, as was occurring with regularity from the early 1980s on. However, the utility of the A–D Line is not in its long-term trend, but in its trend relative to the current bull market. In other words, each time a new bull market begins, the clock is reset for the A–D Line in terms of when it reaches its peak reading. Therefore, divergences are measured, not against the long-term trend of the A–D Line, but against its trend in that particular bull market. This cyclical application has made the A–D Line very useful in forewarning of market tops, not its level relative to the very long-term trend. So it is key to remember that a divergence in the A–D Line is based on its peak reading for the current bull market. It also means a long history of the A–D Line is not necessary to identify a divergence at the next major market top.

Charts created with Metastock, a Thomson Reuters product.

Figure 7.9   The long term downward bias in the NYSE A-D Line, 1957-2005

Cyclical characteristics apply to the NYSE A–D Line, but the same it not true with the A–D Line for another major index—the NASDAQ Comp. As shown in Figure 7.10, there has been little interruption in the downtrend for the NASDAQ A–D Line, a

downtrend that has existed for virtually the entire length of the NAS-
DAQ Comp. Index. This persistent downside bias is due, according to
most analysis, to the inclusion of the many micro-cap stocks traded on
the NASDAQ. Historically, these companies and their stocks fail to
survive for long periods of time. Thus, as these stocks lose their NAS-
DAQ listing, they disappear from the A–D Line, giving it a downward
bias. The end result is NASDAQ's A–D Line fails to provide any useful guidance in terms of signaling the emergence of selective buying
prior to a major top.

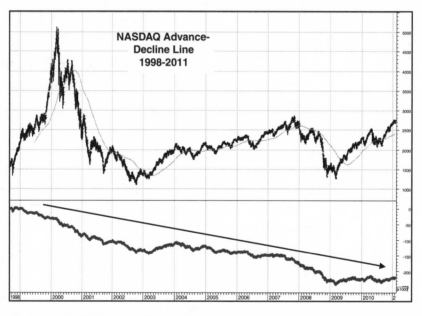

Charts created with Metastock, a Thomson Reuters product.

**Figure 7.10   The long term downward bias in the NASDAQ Comp.
A–D Line**

Another Useful Indicator for Signaling
a Major Market Top

Another means of measuring market breadth, in addition to the
NYSE A–D Line, is the percentage of NY Issues trading above their
30-week moving average. (All examples use a simple, rather than

weighted or exponential moving average.) An A–D Line measures breadth by netting the number of issues that advance or decline on a daily basis, even if an advance is by $0.01. Therefore, an A–D Line provides no indication of the strength of an advance or decline, simply whether more issues rose or fell. An indicator such as the percent of issues above their 30-week moving average (WMA), however, is more a measurement of breadth momentum. In other words, to register as a gain in this indicator, rather than simply closing higher for the day, a stock must move above a benchmark, in this case the 30-WMA. Because a simple 30-WMA is an average of a stock's price over the past 30 weeks, a move above the 30-WMA indicates the stock is now at a level higher than its average price for the past 30 weeks. As such, it could be considered as a measure of strength and upside momentum. In turn, the percentage reading provides an indication of the breadth of the strength and momentum. Typically, in strong rallies, this percentage will steadily rise and confirm new rally highs with highs of its own. Divergences from price highs, however, indicate more selective strength, such as might be experienced as a rally matures and a major top approaches.

This percent indicator, therefore, can act as an important confirming or nonconfirming indicator along with the NYSE A–D Line in signaling the deteriorating strength that typically precedes a major market top. Not only are fewer issues advancing, but more and more stocks are falling below their average prices for the past 30 weeks (about 150 trading days). In addition, the percent indicator is more useful in signaling major market bottoms, while the A–D Line has, historically, provided no indications bear markets were ending.

Because both an A–D Line and a percentage of stocks above a moving average are measures of breadth, it's reasonable to ask why one would work at a market bottom (the percent indicator) while the other does not (the A–D Line). The answer can be found in what each measures. Remember, an A–D Line simply indicates whether a stock rises or falls. The key point here is major market bottoms are not one-time affairs. That is, the bear market doesn't end at one single point and a new bull market begins. As prior chapters show, major market bottoms are a process rather than an event. Thus, a stock may rally in the early phase of the bottoming process only to move lower later on. That move lower registers the stock as a declining component of the A–D Line. However, in rallying, that same stock may cross above a moving average, possibly far enough above so it is able to stay above the moving average even if the stock pulls back later on in the market's bottoming process. As such, it remains in the "above" percentage for the indicator. About any moving average can be used as a benchmark for a percentage stocks indicator. However, a short term moving average could produce many changes in the percentage as both it and the stock display high levels of volatility—that is, it doesn't take much of a price movement for them to shift higher or lower. We have found using a longer term moving average, such as the 30-week, reduces this volatility, thereby generating more reliable signals.

The 30-Week Moving Average in Practice

Every major market top in our study shows a divergence between the major price indexes and the percentage of NY stocks above their 30-WMA. We recommend using both the all-issues NYSE A–D Line and the percent stocks indicator in determining when conditions are developing that indicate a major market top is forming. Apart from adding to the weight of evidence, the 30-WMA also can also provide an indication of the selective strength leading to a major top when the A–D Line does not. For example, Figure 7.11 shows the 1976 market top. Recall there was no A–D Line divergence prior to the end of the 1975–1976 bull market. However, as the chart shows, the percentage of stocks above their 30-WMA began to deteriorate after the peak reading in February 1976, setting two substantially lower highs on rallies in the S&P 500 to the final high in September 1976. Thus although the A–D Line continued to rise, the 30-WMA percentage indicator provided clear evidence of deteriorating strength as the topping process progressed.

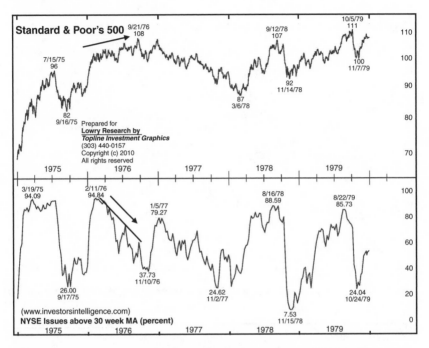

Figure 7.11 The percentage of stocks above their 30-WMA indicator at the 1976 market top

The percentage indicator can, at times, also be a dull instrument in timing a market top, which is why it should be used as a secondary tool, subordinate to the Wyckoff and Lowry analyses of Supply and Demand. For instance, as Figure 7.12 shows, the 30-WMA percent indicator topped in February 1971, a month before the NYSE A–D Line topped in March 1971, both long before the actual market peak in January 1973. Figure 7.13 shows a slightly shorter lead time going into the 2007 market top, as the percentage indicator peaked in December 2006 and then matched that peak in February 2007. The percentage then continued to deteriorate with a sharp drop subsequent to the top in the NYSE A–D Line in early June, suggesting a significantly weakening market condition prior to the rally to their October highs by the major price indexes.

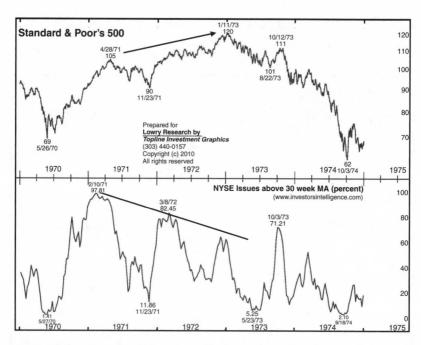

Figure 7.12   The percent stocks indicator prior to the 1973 market top

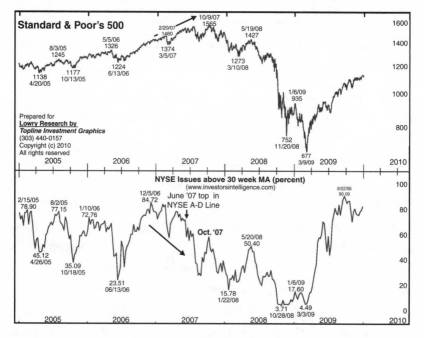

Figure 7.13   The percent stocks indicator at the 2007 market top

Figures 7.14–7.16 illustrate how the 30-WMA percentage indicator can help at major market bottoms. Figure 7.14 shows the market bottom in 1982, where the final low was reached in August. However, the percentage bottomed in September 1981, setting a series of higher lows over the next 11 months, suggesting gradually strengthening market conditions. A similar positive divergence is evident in Figure 7.15 at the July and October 2002 market lows, as the percent indicator is clearly above its July low in October, despite the lower low in prices. Finally, Figure 7.16 shows the most recent market bottom, in 2009, with the percent indicator clearly above its October low at the March price low.

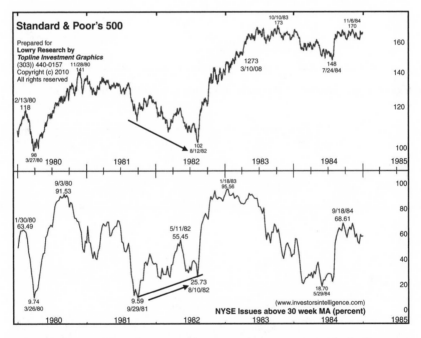

Figure 7.14   Positive divergence between the percent stocks indicator and the S&P 500 at the 1982 market bottom

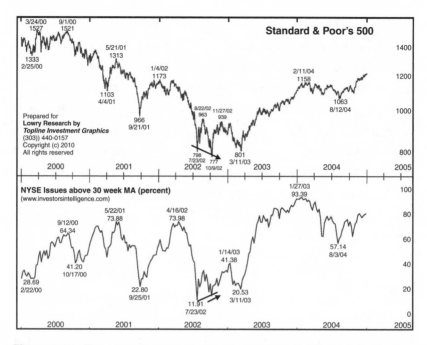

Figure 7.15   The percent stocks indicator at the 2002–2003 market bottom

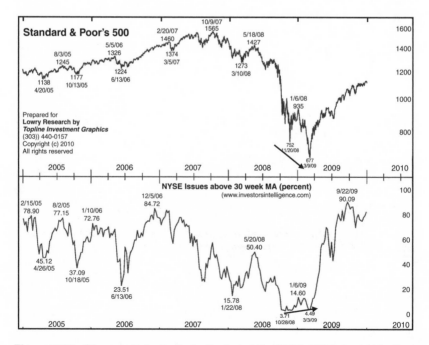

Figure 7.16   The percent stocks indicator at the 2008–2009 market bottom

Conclusion

When doing an analysis of major market tops and bottoms, or for that matter any aspect of stock market behavior, the more indicators that point to the same conclusion, the more accurate the analysis is likely to be. What we have attempted to do in this and the preceding chapters is put together a number of different indicators that, when used together, can provide a reliable guide to market conditions. It is important to remember this is not the same as simply using a lot of indicators. A pitfall of technical analysis is what is called *multicolinearity*, which is a fancy way of saying using a lot of indicators that measure the same thing. For instance, one might use ten different indicators, all of which measure market momentum. It's no surprise that all will probably point to the same conclusion about market conditions. Our intent is aimed at providing a set of indicators that measure different things: the Wyckoff analysis—price/volume activity; the Lowry analysis—Supply and Demand; the A–D Lines—market breadth; and the percentage of stocks above their 30-WMA—a measure of breadth momentum. Used together, these analytical instruments can provide a powerful means for alerting investors about the formation of major market tops and bottoms. And with the ability to identify these key turning points, investors should be able to avoid a "roller coaster to nowhere" of constantly riding bull markets higher and bear markets lower, ending up with very little to show for the ride in terms of increasing portfolio value.

Endnotes

[1] Unless otherwise noted, A–D Line refers to the NYSE Composite Advance–Decline Line.

[2] Charles D. Kirkpatrick and Julie R Dahlquist, *Technical Analysis: The Complete Resource for Financial Market Technicians* (Upper Saddle River, N.J.: FT Press, 2006), p. 130.

[3] Market breadth pertains to the number of advancing versus declining issues in an up or down move in the market, as in the breadth of a market rally or reaction.

8

The Curious Case of the 2000–2001 Market Top and Demise of the Secular Bull Market

In 2007, Nassim Taleb published a book titled *The Black Swan*. The primary theme of the book is the impact of unforeseen events, that is, an event falling outside historical precedents. These so-called outliers can occur in nature, in human society, and in financial markets. Thus, while the Japanese constructed their nuclear power plants to withstand all expected earthquakes, the designers failed to anticipate a 9.0 magnitude quake and subsequent tsunami in March 2011 wiping out all back-up power, setting in motion a chain of events leading to the destruction of these plants. Similarly, the Nobel laureates at Long Term Capital Management did not account for a seismic shift in the bond markets rendering their trading models useless.

Such was also the case with the 2000–2001 market top. While the bubble in technology and Internet stocks was widely acknowledged, the speed at which these stocks crumbled was unanticipated. However, what made the 2000 market top unique was the localized nature of destruction. For example, while the S&P Technology Sector lost over 40% in 2000 alone, other S&P Sectors showed gains comparable to those that might occur in an entire bull market. Because of these unique features, the 2000–2001 market top is clearly different from other market tops discussed. Therefore, this market top, a black swan in its own right, seems to deserve a chapter all its own. The discussion of the 2000–2001 market top may also serve as a cautionary tale to help investors recognize and prepare for those tops that significantly deviate from the historical patterns.

It is generally acknowledged the market top in 2000–2001 marked the end of the great secular bull market that began in 1982 and saw the DJIA rise from a low at 776 in August 1982 to a high at 11,723 in January 2000. The ensuing bear market is regarded as one of the worst since the 1929–32 market plunge. In fact, though, apart from the evisceration of many stocks traded on the NASDAQ Exchange, the 2000–2003 decline represented a relatively modest bear market. And for small- and mid-cap stocks, the bear market was actually a relatively short-lived affair, no worse than the cyclical bear markets in the 1980s and 1990s. In this chapter, we examine what made the 2000–2001 market top and ensuing bear market unique and discuss ways investors might have avoided the worst of the decline.

The Major Market Indexes at the 2000–2001 Top and Ensuing Bear Market

One of the more readily identifiable features of the market top in 2000 was the different times at which the various market indexes peaked. Typically, the major indexes, such as the DJ Industrials, S&P 500, and NASDAQ Comp. tend to peak at about the same time. As Table 8.1 shows, at the 1972–1973 market top, all three of these indexes peaked on the same date—January 11, 1973. The S&P 500 led the way at the 1980–1981 market top, peaking on November 28, 1980, while the NASDAQ Comp. and DJIA peaked within a month of one another, on May 29, 1981, and April 27, 1981, respectively. Similarly, at the 2007 market top, the DJIA and S&P 500 topped on the same date, October 9, 2007, with the NASDAQ Comp. following about three weeks later on October 31, 2007.

TABLE 8.1   Tops in Major Price Indexes

Index	Dates of Bull Market Highs			
	1973	**1980–81**	**2000–2002**	**2007**
DJ Industrials	1/11/1973	4/27/1981	1/14/2000	10/9/2007
S&P 500	1/11/1973	11/28/1980	3/24/2000	10/9/2007
NASDAQ Comp.	1/11/1973	5/29/1981	3/10/2000	10/31/2007
S&P 400 Mid Cap	N/A	N/A	4/16/2002	7/13/2007
S&P 600 Small Cap	N/A	N/A	4/19/2002	7/19/2007

Contrast these performances with the market tops for these same indexes in 2000. The DJIA topped first (Figure 8.1) on January 14, 2000, followed by tops in the NASDAQ Comp. on March 10 and the S&P 500 on March 24. That seems like a reasonable clustering of tops, all within a couple months. That's not the whole story though. As shown in Figure 8.1, while the March top in the NASDAQ Comp. was followed by a steep plunge, the DJIA and S&P 500 traded essentially sideways for the next five months. This sideways trading was followed by a rally in early September that took both the DJIA and S&P 500 back close to their rally peaks from earlier in the year. Specifically, the September 2000 rally took the DJIA back to a peak at 11,310, versus a January 2000 top at 11,723, for a loss of just 3.5%. The September rally took the S&P 500 even closer to its March 2000 peak at 1527, as the Index closed on September 1 2000 at 1520. Contrast this to the NASDAQ Comp., which, at its rally high in September, was at 4234, more than 16% below its March high at 5048.62.

The performances of the S&P Mid and Small Cap Indexes differed even more. Both the Mid and Small Cap Indexes reached rally highs in March 2000 (Figure 8.2). But unlike their big cap counterparts, both Indexes continued to climb throughout the next five months, reaching new rally highs in September significantly above their March levels. Although both the Mid and Small Cap Indexes suffered steep pullbacks in early 2001 and then again in August–September 2001, both were able to recover from these pullbacks to reach new all-time highs. In fact, as seen in Figure 8.2, peak readings in the two Indexes were not reached until April 2002.

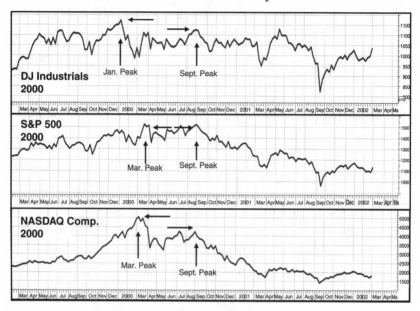

Charts created with Metastock, a Thomson Reuters product.

Figure 8.1   2000 market peaks for the DJIA, S&P 500, and NASDAQ Comp

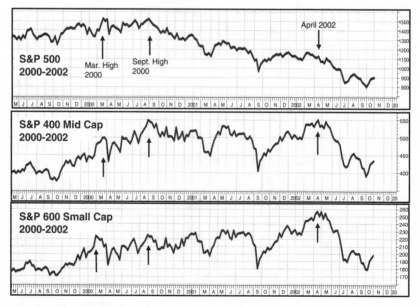

Charts created with Metastock, a Thomson Reuters product.

Figure 8.2   S&P Small and Mid Cap Indexes, 2000-2002

In sum, the 2000–2001 market top, in terms of the performance by the various market indexes, presented a very mixed bag. Both the DJIA and S&P 500 spent most of the year trading sideways, testing their early year highs in September 2000. The S&P Mid and Small Cap Indexes performed even better, reaching new rally highs in September 2000. The NASDAQ Comp. was the only one of the major indexes showing a sharp decline throughout the year. Thus, in terms of losses in the major price indexes, up until the market highs in September, there really wasn't much of a bear market at all during 2000, except, of course, for the implosion of the tech stock bubble where the impact was felt most acutely in the NASDAQ Comp. The diverse performances of the major market indexes was the first major difference between the 2000 market top and prior major market tops. The different performances also highlights the dangers of liquidating portfolios in response to the losses shown by the NASDAQ Index. In fact, this would have been exactly the wrong thing to do for portfolios invested in small and mid cap stocks outside the technology and telecommunications sectors and only slightly less damaging for big cap portfolios invested outside the bubble stocks.

Thus, a key differentiating feature of the 2000–2003 bear was the unequal distribution of losses. The sell-off was obviously painful for investors with heavy exposure to technology issues, as reflected by the nearly 78% loss in the NASDAQ Comp. But for investors who were either astute (lucky?) enough to exit their tech stocks near the top, or for those who avoided those stocks altogether, the 2000–2003 bear was a much less momentous affair, with losses in the DJIA and S&P 500 at 37.8% and 49.2%, respectively. In fact, the loss in the DJIA was not that much more than the average bear market decline of 32.2% from 1940 to 2000. And, for those fortunate enough to have large exposure to mid and small cap stocks, the 2000–2003 bear was a relatively short-lived (April–October 2002) and limited decline with the S&P Small Cap Index down 33.78% and the Mid Cap Index down

32.25%. In other words, there were plenty of places to hide in the 2000–2003 bear market to limit the damage to an investor's portfolio.

In contrast, there was no place to hide during the 2007–2009 bear market. While the major market indexes showed a wide range of losses in the 2000–2003 bear decline, the opposite was true of the sell-off from October 2007 to March 2009. In this case, there was nowhere to hide, as the range of losses shown by the major indexes was so narrow as to be almost invisible. As Table 8.2 shows, all the major indexes—big, mid, and small—had losses within a few percentage points of one another, with the DJIA holding up best (if holding up is even applicable), while the S&P Small Cap Index ended with the largest loss. However, all were within the 50% range, while the same indexes showed losses during the 2000–2003 bear ranging from nearly 78% to just over 32%.

TABLE 8.2   Losses of Major Indexes 2007–2009

DJ Industrials	-53.78%
S&P 500	-56.78%
NASDAQ Comp.	-55.63%
S&P 400 Mid Cap	-56.30%
S&P 600 Small Cap	-59.17%

At this point, our reader might be asking, so market indexes topped at different times and showed widely different losses during the 2000–2003 bear market. How does this apply to identifying a major market top? Well, with indexes topping all over the place and with some showing losses of more than double others, using an analysis of just one major price index to define the market top could produce misleading results. In the case of the 2000–2003 top, it might be fair to ask regarding the major market indexes, which top are you referring to? The NASDAQ top in March 2000, the S&P 500 in September 2000, or maybe the S&P Small Cap top in April 2002? All of them would require their own analysis, and each would produce different results in terms of the subsequent bear trend. We try to partially resolve this conundrum by looking at the two indexes that were, in all likelihood, the most closely watched—the NASDAQ Comp. and S&P 500—and apply our analysis to the tops in those two indexes. But for now, we turn our attention to two other complexities of the 2000 market top, beginning with market breadth.

The 2000–2001 Market Top and the NYSE Advance–Decline Line

As noted in Chapter 7, Advance–Decline Lines have, historically, been one of the most useful indicators in warning of approaching major market tops. They accomplish this warning through divergences. That is, while the major price indexes are rallying to a series of new bull market highs, the A–D Lines record a series of lower peaks, or, in other words, diverge from the action of the price indexes. Historically, these divergences have occurred, on average, about 7 months prior to major market tops. However, this average includes some outliers, including a 17-month lead time prior to the 1968–1969 market top and, most significantly, a 23-month lead prior to the 2000–2001 market top. This nearly 2-year lead time has led some analysts to conclude the NYSE Composite Advance–Decline Line (A–D Line), which is the indicator most often used in signaling these divergences, was, in this case, almost worthless as a timing tool in terms of warning of the market's final top. And in this case, as a timing tool, the A–D Line does appear of little use in identifying the ultimate market top. That said, the behavior of the A–D Line is another piece of the unusual character of the 2000–2001 market top, and as such, its behavior carries some useful information about what was going on in the stock market prior to the end of the bull market—information that could prove valuable in identifying a future anomalous market top.

The 23-month lag between the high in the A–D Line and, in this case, the DJIA, dated to April 1998, which ended a long uptrend in the A–D Line dating to early 1995. As shown in Figure 8.3, Point A, though, in one sense, the A–D Line did act as an accurate predictor of a bull market top—the July 1998 market high, which was followed by the 3-month bear market that ended in October 1998. So far, so good. The A–D Line bottomed in October, along with the major price indexes, right on schedule. However, rather than starting a new uptrend, the A–D Line rose for only about a month before renewing its downtrend. Clearly, something different was going on. Had the market indexes also turned lower, the decline in the A–D Line would have been of little consequence. But, as history shows, all the major indexes rebounded from the October 1998 lows into a new bull market that lasted for almost the next two years.

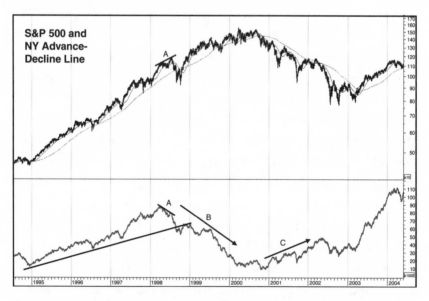

Charts created with Metastock, a Thomson Reuters product.

Figure 8.3   The NYSE A–D Line leading up to the 2000 market top

Generally, the steady downtrend in the A–D Line from late 1998 to early 2000 (Figure 8.3 Point B) is laid at the feet of the dot-com bubble in technology stocks. That is, many investors rushed into these technology and dot-com stocks at the expense of stocks in just about any other industry sector. However, the tech bubble burst with the top in the NASDAQ Comp. in March, 2000. That top was matched by a top in the S&P 500 in March and preceded by the January 2000 top in the DJIA. The tops in the DJIA and S&P 500 were tested in September 2000, and it was only then all three indexes dropped into a clearly defined bear trend. But here's where it gets interesting. As shown in Figure 8.3, rather than joining the market indexes in a bear trend, the A–D Line actually *bottomed* in October 2000 and began an uptrend that lasted nearly 18 months, until May 2002 (Figure 8.3, Point C). To understand why, we need to first go back to the downtrend in the A–D Line from late 1998 to early 2000 when all the price indexes were rallying.

The lag in the A–D Line during those 14 months from 1998 to 2000 was due primarily to investor infatuation with all things dot-com plus those fellow-traveler stocks in the telecom and, to a lesser extent, consumer discretionary and industrial sectors. For example, even though the broad market indexes (and the DJIA) rallied after the 1998 bear market, two industry sectors, Consumer Staples and Healthcare, never recovered. Instead, both stayed in downtrends right up to early 2000 (Figure 8.4). Similarly, other sectors, such as Energy, Finance, and Basic Materials, had very erratic performances over this 14-month period, alternating between sharp rallies and equally sharp moves lower. Thus, there were clearly a number of areas of broad-based weakness that account for the lag in the A–D Line going into the 2000 market top. Renewed strength in these lagging sectors also helps explain what proved to be a very selective market in 2000 and the recovery by the DJIA and S&P 500 later in the year back almost to their early year highs.

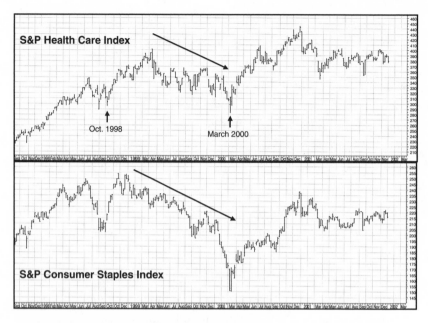

Charts created with Metastock, a Thomson Reuters product.

Figure 8.4   Performances of the healthcare and consumer staples sectors 1998–2000

The Ten S&P Industry Sectors and the Market Top

Not only did the S&P industry sectors play a role in explaining the performance of the A–D Line prior to the 2000 market top, but they also played a very significant role in how the major market top formed in 2000–2001.

In the first section of this chapter, we discussed the different performances of the major price indexes in terms of when they peaked and how they behaved through the balance of 2000. In large part, the difference in performance between the DJIA, S&P 500, and NASDAQ Comp. can be attributed to gains and losses in the various S&P industry sectors.

Except for those investors and traders caught up in the dot.com/telecom frenzy, the year 2000 was not all that bad and, in one or two instances, relatively good. This much is evident in the performances of the ten S&P industry sectors for the year. We go into the exact timing of tops for the industry sectors a little later in this chapter, but for now their performances for the year can serve as an indication of how uneven returns were for 2000. Table 8.3 lists the gains/losses for the ten sectors from December 31, 1999, to December 29, 2000. As the table shows, for investors in Info Tech, Telecom, or Consumer Discretionary stocks, 2000 was a very bad year. On the other hand, investors holding utility stocks had every right to question, "What bear market?" with the Sector up by over 50%. Other than these extreme gains and losses, the performances of the remaining industry sectors varied from modest gains to modest losses. But with only four of the ten sectors showing losses for 2000, it would be very difficult to classify the year as a nasty bear market.

TABLE 8.3 **Performance of Ten S&P Industry Sectors 12/31/99–12/29/00**

Sector	Percent Gain/Loss
Basic Materials	-17.70%
Consumer Staples	14.50%
Consumer Discretionary	-20.70%
Energy	13.20%
Finance	23.40%
Healthcare	35.50%
Industrials	4.50%
Info Tech	-41%
Telecommunications	-36.60%
Utilities	51.70%

Another way of looking at the performances of these industry sectors as they applied to the bear market is when they actually reached their peaks for the 1998–2000 bull market. Of the ten sectors, only two topped in 2000: Basic Materials in January and Info Tech in March. Two sectors reached their bull market peaks in 1999: Telecom in July and Consumer Discretionary in December. The other six sectors either peaked in 2001 (Finance in January, Utilities in April, and Energy and Industrials in May) or not until 2002 (Healthcare in

March and Consumer Staples in May). In Figure 8.5, we plotted the points at which each industry sector topped relative to the S&P 500 Index in 1999–2002. As is evident, there is little uniformity in terms of when these sectors descended into bear trends.

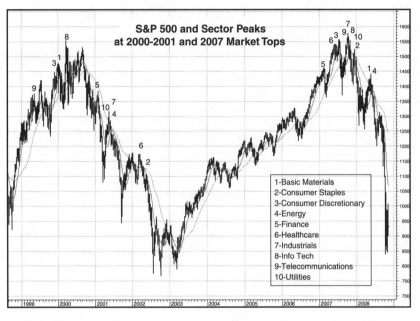

Charts created with Metastock, a Thomson Reuters product.

Figure 8.5   Timing of industry sector bull market peaks at the 2000 and 2007 market tops

But might this scattered timing of rally highs for the sectors be the norm for major market tops? An examination of the 2007 market top suggests the answer to that question is no. Table 8.4 shows the times when each of the ten S&P industry sectors peaked at the 2007 market top. With the exception of the Finance Sector, which topped in February 2007 and the Energy and Basic Materials Sectors, which topped in May 2008, the peaks for the industry sectors were clustered either at or just prior to the July highs in the market indexes and at or slightly after the October 2007 peaks in the market indexes. This pattern is far different from the one at the 2000 market top, where the bull market highs for the ten sectors were scattered over a period of nearly three years, from the top in Telecom in July 1999 to the May

2002 top in Consumer Staples. Figure 8.5 illustrates the difference of the peaks in the S&P Sectors at the 2000 and 2007 market tops.

TABLE 8.4   Industry Sectors Tops in 2007–2008

Sector	Date Topped
Basic Materials	May 16, 2008
Consumer Staples	Dec 10, 2007
Cons. Discretionary	Jun 4, 2007
Energy	May 20, 2008
Finance	Feb 20, 2007
Healthcare	May 7, 2007
Industrials	Oct 9, 2007
Info Tech	Oct 31, 2007
Telecommunications	Sep 27, 2007
Utilities	Dec 10, 2007

In terms of when the most widespread damage was done in the 2000–2003 bear market, it seems clear the worst of the decline occurred from April 2002, when the small and mid cap indexes topped, to the reaction low in October 2002. There seems little reason to question the view the 2000 market top marked the end of the secular bull market that began in 1982. However, in terms of when the most damage was done in the 2000–2003 bear market, the six-month period between April and October 2002 seemed to have much in common with the cyclical bear markets in 1987, 1990, and 1998, each of which lasted three–four months. So if the end of the secular bull market is based on when the most widespread and long-lasting damage was done, then the 2007–2009 bear market might mark a better ending point for the secular bull that began in 1982.

That more widespread damage was done in the 2007–2009 bear market than during the 2000–2003 bear appears borne out by the losses suffered by the S&P industry sectors. Table 8.5 compares the losses for each of the ten S&P sectors in the 2000–2003 and 2007–2009 bear markets. The average loss during the 2007–2009 bear was 55.14% with a median loss of 54.7%. In contrast, the average loss in the 2000–2003 bear market was 49.24% with a median loss of 43.7%. Clearly, the most significant damage in the 2000–2003 bear was limited to the Info Tech and Telecom sectors, while damage was more equally distributed in the 2007–2009 bear. The exception in this most recent bear market was the Financial Sector, which actually suffered a larger loss—83.96%—than the loss of 82.51% by the Tech Sector in the 2000–2003 bear. In fact, though, severe losses were probably more widespread in the tech stock meltdown when many of the dot-com stocks simply disappeared. The big drop in the Finance Sector in the 2007–2009 bear was more likely due to the evisceration of big cap names in the banking (Citicorp, Bank of America), insurance (AIG), and brokers/investment banking (Lehman Bros., Bear Sterns, Merrill Lynch) than to the disappearance of wide swaths of financial stocks.

TABLE 8.5   Losses for the Ten S&P Industry Sectors in the Bear Markets

Sector	2000–2003	2007–2009
Basic Materials	-39.74%	-60.09%
Consumer Staples	-26.00%	-34.84%
Consumer Discretionary	-45.39%	-60.53%
Energy	-35.67%	-54.43%
Finance	-38.32%	-83.96%
Healthcare	-42.03%	-40.57%
Industrials	-45.70%	-65.15%
Info Tech	-82.51%	-55.02%
Telecommunications	-73.68%	-47.61%
Utilities	-63.40%	-49.17%
Average Loss	-49.24%	55.14%
Median Loss	-43.70%	54.70%

Given the disparity in the timing of bull market tops for the various price indexes, and the even greater dispersion of peaks for the various industry sectors, when discussing the 2000 market top, as noted earlier it might be fair to ask, "Which market did you have in mind?" For that reason, in the next chapter, we split our analysis of the 2000 market top in terms of the application of the Wyckoff and Lowry principles, into two parts. First, we look at the market top for the S&P 500 and then follow with an analysis of the top for the NAS-DAQ Comp. Index. Although both indexes bottomed at the same time and in about the same way, their tops looked nothing alike. Consequently, it seems appropriate each top deserves its own examination. Although we use the Buying Power and Selling Pressure Indexes in our examination of the 2000 top in the S&P 500, these Indexes are not currently calculated for the NASDAQ Comp. Index. Consequently, we rely strictly on the Wyckoff analysis in our study of the NASDAQ Comp. in 2000. One final note: Although the DJIA has been used for our prior studies, given the disparities in performance between the DJIA and the other major indexes, the S&P 500 appears to offer a better proxy for the 2000–2001 market top.

9

A Wyckoff/Lowry Analysis of the 2000 Market Top

The 2000–2001 Market Top According to the S&P 500

It's springtime 1999, and all seems right in the stock market. Tech stocks and, in particular, just about anything associated with the Internet are making overnight millionaires. Analysts are projecting the sky's the limit for earnings, the economy is strong, and grandmothers have turned into day-traders to make a little extra cash and maybe strike it rich. But over the summer, observant investors notice something troubling. The rally in the S&P 500 stalls in mid-July, and on the following pullback into mid-October, something unusual happens. NYSE volume shows a distinct rise as the pullback proceeds. At the same time, the Selling Pressure Index begins to rise, in the process breaking a downtrend dating to October 1998 and suggesting sellers are becoming more active (Figure 9.1). These observant investors are likely already aware of the, by now, protracted decline in the NYSE Advance–Decline Line, warning of a narrowing rally. The lack of breadth behind the rally is also indicated by a drop in the percent of NYSE stocks trading above their 30-week moving average (Figure 9.2).

Charts created with Metastock, a Thomson Reuters product.

Figure 9.1   S&P 500; buying power and selling pressure

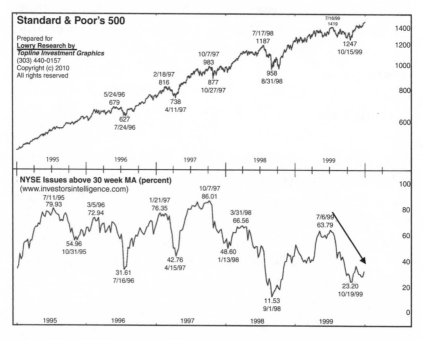

Figure 9.2   S&P 500; percent of NYSE issues trading above their 30-WMA

Taken together, the rise in volume and Selling Pressure, plus the divergence by the A–D Line and percent of NYSE stocks above their 30-week moving average suggested the July–October market decline was an indication of Preliminary Supply (PSY).

However, the final push lower in the July–October pullback resulted in prices falling to an area of possible Demand at the January–February trading range (not shown). Buyers who missed out on the rally following that trading range evidently did not want to miss another opportunity, as prices rebounded in an advance that lasted into the end of December. But a couple strange things happened on this rally. Although the S&P 500 continued higher on heavy volume in late November and early October, Selling Pressure began to rise and Buying Power to fall (Point A on Figure 9.3). Volume subsequently dried up dramatically in late December, as was usual due to seasonal factors.

Charts created with Metastock, a Thomson Reuters product.

Figure 9.3   S&P 500 at the 2000–2001 market top

As a result, there was no evidence of any sort of Buying Climax at the market top in early January 2000. However, rather than staying light on the pullback in early January 2000, volume rose sharply, suggesting a significant unloading of stock, characteristic of an Automatic Reaction. But, again, buyers stepped in when prices fell back to support at the sideways trading of late November/early December, producing a rally on continued heavy volume. Despite the heavy volume, this rally failed to move above the highs reached in early January—signs of a Secondary Test (ST). When the rally failed at the early January 2000 high, prices once again turned lower. But volume remained heavy, and Selling Pressure continued to rise on this pullback, suggesting investors were again aggressively unloading stock—a sign of distribution.

After a few days of heavy trading in late February failed to send prices lower (Point B in Figure 9.3), buyers jumped back in. The result was a renewed rally on rising volume that included, on March 16, a 90% Up Day, suggesting buying was reaching panic proportions. But volume quickly dried up, as buyers evidently began having second thoughts about chasing the rally. The result was a short-lived higher high, which quickly failed, characteristic of an Upthrust after Distribution (UAD). After a sharp spike lower in early April failed to hold, a brief effort was made to restart the rally. This proved a weak attempt, as the rally failed below the level of the Upthrust high. This failed rally evidently exaggerated fears the tech bubble was about to burst because selling quickly reached panic proportions with a 90% Down Day on April 14 (Point C) that took prices back to the level of the February and March market lows. But that 90% Down Day evidently temporarily exhausted Supply. At the same time, the Demand that sent prices higher from the February–March lows was evidently still present, resulting in a quick rally.

Despite the rally from the mid-April low, there seems to be ample evidence that buyers were becoming wary of the rally. Thus far, though, the selling had appeared selective and focused on the formerly high-flying technology and Internet stocks on the NASDAQ Exchange. For example, while tech stocks were plummeting, stocks in other industry sectors, such as Utilities, Consumer Staples, Finance or Energy, were holding up rather well. The result was, while the NASDAQ Comp. was moving lower, the S&P 500 entered into a trading range beginning in late April and lasting to late August. The question at this point was whether this trading range represented a period of accumulation or distribution. After all, the plunge in the tech stocks might have served as a safety valve for the market in general, as the excesses were purged, allowing the remainder of the market to resume its rally.

The problem with positive expectations for the S&P 500's trading range was evident in the performances of Buying Power and Selling Pressure. Apparently, there was little urgency to sell (outside the tech stocks), as Selling Pressure began a slow decline, lasting to September. But at the same time, buyers appeared content to sit on the sidelines, as Buying Power also went into a slow decline.

However, this relatively benign relationship between Supply and Demand was about to change. The S&P 500 made another run at the March highs in mid July 2000, with the rally failing just below the March peak. However, on the subsequent pullback, volume showed a small rise, suggesting sellers were again becoming more aggressive. Any worries about the rise in volume on this pullback were likely compounded by the ensuing August rally, as volume went into a steady decline. This drop in volume may have been seasonal in nature (the summer doldrums), but the apparent lack of Demand left the rally vulnerable to any rise in Supply. And that rise in Supply was forthcoming as the rally to early September 2000 failed slightly above the July high, as there were evidently still plenty of sellers left around that July level. This September high also included a minor buying climax on August 31 (Point D). This panic buying, plus the failure around the July high, gave the rally the characteristics of a Terminal Upthrust (TU).

From this point, the bull market from the 1998 low quickly unraveled. Selling accelerated on the decline in September, with both volume and Selling Pressure steadily rising—evidence of a Sign of Weakness decline (SOW). After a few days of hesitation in late September 2000, the S&P 500 broke sharply lower on October 6 (Point E) in a Break through the Ice. But, once again, prices found support around the levels of the February and April lows. The resulting rebound rally, though, showed only a minimal rise in Buying Power and virtually no loss in Selling Pressure, suggesting active selling into the advance. The rally then failed when it reached the overhead resistance provided by the late September trading range, having retraced less than half the decline from the September high. All this was characteristic of a Last Point of Supply (LPSY). When the decline following the LPSY dropped below support at the February, April, and October lows, it was evident the bear market was now fully underway.

The 2000 Market Top and Bursting of the Bubble in the NASDAQ Comp. Index

The 2000 top for the S&P 500 was a drawn-out process of attrition, but the pain was much more immediate for investors in NAS-DAQ tech stocks. However, the bull market continued for slightly longer on the NASDAQ, as the Index cruised right along with barely a ripple during the July to October 1999 pullback in the S&P 500. About the worst that can be said is prices moved generally sideways over this period. The NASDAQ Comp. then went into another steep rally with barely any hiccups, at least until early January 2000.

During the first week in January and then again during the latter part of the month, the NASDAQ Comp. Index, however, suffered its first noticeable pullback since late July 1999. What's more, volume remained relatively heavy on both the early and late January declines. Given what was happening elsewhere in the market, especially with the S&P 500, an alert investor would likely have recognized a possible point of Preliminary Supply (PSY, Figure 9.4). The pause was only temporary, though, as prices again accelerated into another rally on generally rising volume. On March 7, 2000 (Point A), prices surged to a new all-time high on heavy volume. But the rally failed to hold, as the NASDAQ Comp. closed near its low for the day and below the prior two days' closes. That's not a bad description of a Buying Climax. Buyers were little dissuaded, as prices quickly rebounded into a renewed move higher. Volume was diminished on this rally, however, which ended on March 10 (Point B) with another spike to a new high although the NASDAQ Comp. closed near its low for the day. This final new high proved to be the last gasp for the bull run in the NAS-DAQ, though the topping pattern still had several more months to fully play out.

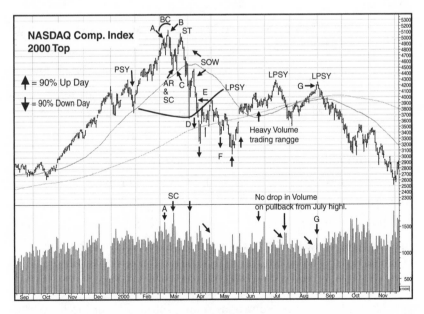

Charts created with Metastock, a Thomson Reuters product.

Figure 9.4   NASDAQ Composite Index at the 2000 market top

Following the March 10 high, prices swiftly moved lower over the next few days, with volume again reaching climax proportions on March 16, 2000. In this case, the climax was of the selling variety. Given that the apparent Selling Climax (SC) followed a decline of only three days, investors would have rightly questioned its longer term significance. Nevertheless, the level of selling on the pullback to the March 16 low was heavy enough to classify the decline as an Automatic Reaction. Any prognosis that a rebound following the March 16 SC could be short-lived proved accurate, as the rally lasted only one day and was followed by test of the SC low on March 21 (Point C). Volume on this test was much diminished from volume on the SC, suggesting Supply had, at least temporarily, been exhausted.

Prices did, indeed, rebound, but again the rally lasted only three days and served largely as a test of the March 16 high, labeling it as a likely Secondary Test (ST). Volume on the test, though, was substantially less than volume at the March 16 high, suggesting weakening Demand, as buyers were becoming increasingly reluctant to chase prices higher. When prices failed to punch through to new highs, selling again accelerated on a steady rise in volume. The drop from the ST culminated in another apparent SC on April 4 (Point D) on slightly more volume than the March 16 SC. But as was the case in March, the April 5 SC evidently served to only temporarily exhaust Supply, as the subsequent rebound rally failed after only three days.

At this point, it was becoming clear sellers were establishing themselves as the dominant force in the market, using any rebound as an opportunity to unload stock. The speed, expanding daily range and volume of the decline from the late March 2000 high, therefore, appeared to fulfill the requirements of a Sign of Weakness (SOW) decline. About all that was left now was for a break through final support, or a Break through the Ice in Wyckoff terms. The stage was quickly set for this breakdown, as selling intensified in the form of a 90% Down Day on April 12 (Point E), on the approach to key support at the low of the April 4 SC. The actual Break through the Ice occurred on a gap lower and a second 90% Down Day on April 14.

Frequently a second 90% Down Day, occurring quickly after the first, serves to at least temporarily exhaust Supply. And that was the case this time, as the NASDAQ Comp. rebounded over the next couple weeks. However, our alert investor probably noticed volume on this rebound failed to show any significant expansion. To the contrary, volume actually declined—action typical of a rally to the Last Point of Supply (LPSY). This LPSY also served as a test of the Break through the Ice, suggesting the topping process was complete and the NASDAQ Comp. was now ready to fall into a full-fledged bear trend.

Indications the topping process was complete appeared reinforced by yet another 90% Down Day on May 10 (Point F). Although the NASDAQ Comp. quickly recovered, the rebound proved short-lived, as prices again turned lower after running into minor resistance at the four-day trading range from early May 2000. But volume failed to show any significant increase on the subsequent decline, suggesting sellers were in short supply, a suggestion reinforced when prices rebounded from a test of the mid-April low. Hopes the worst was over for die-hard bulls were rekindled in the form of two 90% Up Days (May 30 and June 2) on the rebound rally. These hopes were reinforced when, after a brief hesitation around the level of the April LPSY, prices broke out to the upside. The breakout proved short-lived, as prices fell back during the latter part of June 2000. However, heavy volume during the sideways trading in late June failed to produce any further decline (Wyckoff's Law of Effort vs. Result), suggesting Demand was increasing. Once again, though, as prices rallied in early July, volume failed to show any significant expansion. The lack of volume suggested this rally represented another move to a LPSY (remember, despite the name, there can be more than one LPSY), especially since the rally failed at the level of the February 2000 reaction lows and just below the early April 2000 rebound high.

The ensuing pullback from the mid-July high and rally to the late August 2000 peak was the proverbial "two-by-four upside the head" for any die-hard, holdout bulls that the great NASDAQ bull market of the past two years was over.

First, volume failed to show any noticeable contraction on the pullback from the mid-July high, suggesting sellers were content to get what they could and were unwilling to wait for higher prices. Second, volume then decreased markedly on the rally to the late August high, further suggesting willing buyers were becoming a disappearing breed. The coup de grace was a final spike higher in volume in an apparent two-day buying climax on August 31 and September 1, 2000 (Point G). Despite the spike in volume, the rally failed to move above the mid July high, as sellers took over. Had the rally to the September high represented a resurrected bull market, the advance should have easily moved to new recovery highs. The fact the rebound failed at almost exactly the same level as the July rebound high, however, suggested another LPSY was reached. The subsequent decline in prices on steadily rising volume provided compelling evidence chances for a rejuvenated bull market were nil. And, indeed, it was from this September high (which corresponded to the rebound highs in the DJ Industrials and S&P 500) that the bear market began in earnest, with a subsequent drop in the NASDAQ Comp. from its September 1, 2000, rally high at 4234 to its final low at 1114 on October 9, 2002.

The 2000–2001 market top was, in many if not most aspects, a unique event in terms of the formation of bull market tops. Apart from technology stocks and a few others in sectors, such as Consumer Discretionary and Telecommunications, the year 2000 was relatively good for many investors. However, even sectors that were higher in 2000 eventually fell victim to the wave of selling that engulfed the tech stocks in 2000. Though this uneven distribution of selling rendered reliable tools for indicating market tops, such as the NYSE A–D Line or the Percent of NY Stocks above their 30-week moving average, less useful as timing instruments, an examination of the major price indexes, using the Wyckoff tools for price/volume analysis and measures of Supply and Demand, allowed investors to recognize the features that have, historically, identified major market tops.

One last note—there is at least one school of thought suggesting the techniques of the "old masters" have been rendered obsolete by changes in the market's structure. This school contends dark pools, flash trading, decimalized quotes, among other things, have changed the character of the market to the extent that more up-to-date tools are needed for a useful analysis. Yet, the methods used in our analyses originated nearly 100 years ago. These methods worked then, and they appear to have worked right through the most recent market bottom in 2009. We can safely assume that market conditions have been in constant flux over this 100 years. Yet these methods still work. Why? Probably because they are reliable, time-tested methods for gauging fear and greed, and the forces of Supply and Demand, none of which have changed over the millennium and aren't likely to change.

10 Where Are We Now?

As discussed in earlier chapters, the most recent major market bottom began forming in the fourth quarter of 2008 and was finalized with the establishment of the March 2009 low. The subsequent bull market, which evolved from that low, remains in force as of this writing in February 2011 and, at present, there is a lack of evidence indicating a major top is close at hand. Before discussing why a continued primary uptrend in the stock market appears likely in the months ahead, we first examine the life of the bull market thus far.

The Bull Market

As the major market indexes embarked on a sustained primary uptrend following the establishment of the final low in the 2008–2009 major market bottom, Lowry's measures of the intermediate-term trends of Supply and Demand, Selling Pressure and Buying Power, acted in a manner uncharacteristic of a market in the midst of a new bull trend. During the initial stage of a new bull market, Selling Pressure typically drops at about the same rate as Buying Power rises, showing that Supply is being withdrawn at the same rate investor Demand is expanding.

In the case of the rally off the March 2009 low, however, there was a clear sluggishness in the contraction of Selling Pressure, as shown in Figure 10.1 (Point A). Specifically, in the month following the March 9 low, Buying Power increased 65 points while Selling

Pressure declined 31 points, less than half the increase in Buying
Power. This sluggishness in Selling Pressure persisted over the subsequent month. And as of May 8, 2009, Selling Pressure was just 34
points below its March 2009 peak, while Buying Power had risen 76
points from its equivalent low (Point B). One viable explanation for
the sluggishness in the contraction of Selling Pressure was investors'
lack of faith in the advance. Given the severity of the preceding bear
market, sellers remained active during the initial advance from the
March 2009 bottom, unwilling to believe that preceding carnage of
the 2007–2009 bear market had fully played itself out.

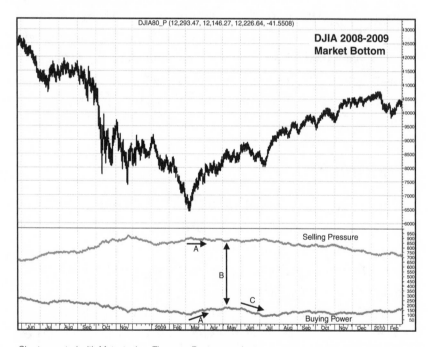

Charts created with Metastock, a Thomson Reuters product.

Figure 10.1   The 2008–2009 major market bottom and subsequent Bull Market

Following this two-month period of rapidly expanding Demand
and sluggishly contracting Supply, concern regarding the sustainabil-
ity of the uptrend apparently increased, as Buying Power, following
its former brisk expansion, began to erode. This erosion began in
early June 2009, (Point C), just as the market was in the process of

forming a corrective top that eventually led to a month-long pullback in the market. During this decline, Buying Power fell 77 points and broke below the 96 reading recorded at the March 2009 bear market low. Thus, confidence in the new bull market diminished further still.

Nonetheless, the internal weakness implied by the sluggish contraction in Supply and subsequent drop in Demand never fully played out in the actions of the major market indexes, as the March 2009 low was never challenged. This was the first time in Lowry's history, which dates back to 1933, where such an extensive rally occurred with the Buying Power Index dropping to new lows. It is also important to note that this was also the first time in Lowry's history where a five-month rally occurred on persistently contracting volume. The contraction in volume, as well as the market pullback into the July low, helped account for the decline in Buying Power. This contraction of volume is clearly evident in Figure 10.2, the 30-day moving average of NYSE Up Volume plus Down Volume.

Charts created with Metastock, a Thomson Reuters product.

Figure 10.2   S&P 500 and 30-day moving average of NYSE Composite Up Volume plus Down Volume

Note that this volume data is compiled using total NYSE Composite Volume, not merely NYSE floor volume. With the growing role of off-exchange trading, using only floor volume probably no longer paints quite an accurate picture of trading activity. Total Composite Volume, however, takes into account all sources outside the floor of the Exchange, including dark pools.

Despite the anomalies of the initial stages of the new bull trend, the market stabilized in early July 2009, and during the subsequent advance, conditions began to appear more typical of a market in the midst of a new primary advance. To quote an excerpt from Lowry's weekly *Primary Trend Perspective* published on August 7, 2009, "...measures of Supply, Demand and volume all appear to be strengthening, which is more consistent with a sustainable rally."

The primary uptrend forged on throughout the third and fourth quarters of 2009. It was not until January 2010 that a correction developed which appeared to threaten the uptrend in place since the July 2009 low. The pullback got off to a rather harrowing start, with the Dow Jones Industrial Average producing four triple-digit declines in the span of five sessions. And two of those declines were in excess of 200 points. All told, that decline, which persisted from January 19, 2010, through February 8, 2010, shaved 7.6% off the Dow Jones Industrial Average.

Although the health of the primary uptrend may have been called into question by some as the early 2010 sell-off persisted, it was the condition of the market prior to that decline that suggested the pullback did not represent the start of a major move lower. First, as shown in Figure 10.3, at the January 19 market high, Selling Pressure remained in a downtrend, having recorded its lowest reading since the bull market began in March 2009. Over Lowry's 78-year history encompassing 18 bull market tops since 1937, there is not a single instance of Selling Pressure recording a new low at a major market peak. In contrast, Selling Pressure tends to establish a well-defined uptrend several months prior to a major market top, reflecting the increased selling that occurs in the latter stages of a bull market.

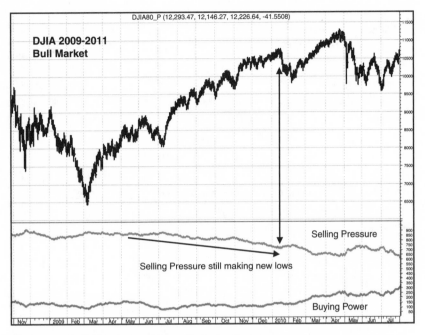

Charts created with Metastock, a Thomson Reuters product.

Figure 10.3   DJIA Bull Market confirmed by Buying Power and Selling Pressure

Market breadth also indicated the early 2010 decline did not represent the beginning of the end of the bull market. As discussed in Chapter 7, "Indentifying Major Tops and Bottoms: Other Tools to Consider," buying tends to diminish while selective selling starts to emerge during the formation of major market tops. These factors become evident in the various market indexes' Advance–Decline Lines, which fail to confirm the new rally highs in their underlying price indexes. However, at the January 19, 2010 market top, the NYSE Composite all-issues, NYSE Operating Companies Only, S&P 500, S&P Mid Cap and NASDAQ Comp. A–D Lines all confirmed the new highs reached by their respective price indexes. Figure 10.4 depicts the A–D Lines of the NYSE Comp. Index as well as NYSE Operating Company Only Index. Given the lack of supporting evidence a major market top had been reached, the probabilities appeared to favor an eventual resumption of the bull market after the correction ran its course.

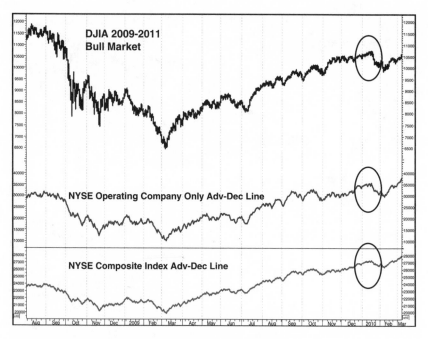

Charts created with Metastock, a Thomson Reuters product.

Figure 10.4   NYSE all-issues and operating company only A–D Lines

Indeed, the market recovered steadily from the February 8 low and by March 17, 2010, had established a new closing high for the bull market. This advance continued virtually uninterrupted until the next intermediate-term top on April 26, 2010. It was the sell-off following this high that tested the mettle of those investors holding long positions in favor an ongoing bull market.

Specifically, during the nine-day decline from the April 26 high through the May 7 close, volume surged, three 90% Downside Days developed, and the Dow Jones Industrial Average lost in excess of 800 points, for a total percentage decline of 7.4%. During this period, the infamous "Flash Crash" occurred (Figure 10.5). This cascade of selling on the afternoon of May 6, 2010 resulted, at one point, in a nearly 1000 point loss on the day in the Dow Jones Industrial Average. Although the precise cause of the debacle is yet to be conclusively determined, generalized blame has been placed on computerized high frequency trading, as noted in a subsequent report resulting from a joint investigation by the U.S. Securities and Exchange Commission (SEC) and the Commodity Futures Trading Commission (CFTC).[1]

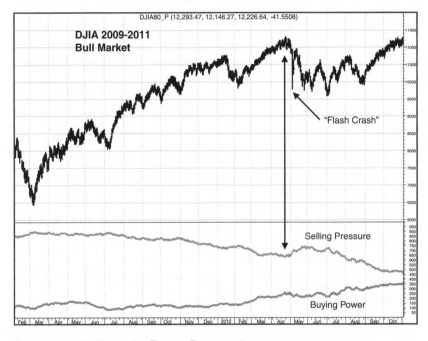

Charts created with Metastock, a Thomson Reuters product.

Figure 10.5   DJIA along with Buying Power and Selling Pressure during May 2010 "Flash Crash"

Although the market rebounded following the flash crash, it would not be until nearly six months later, in early November 2010, that the bull market finally resumed. During the period from late April through November 2010, skepticism regarding the market's ability to resume the bull trend abounded. This was not surprising, considering that at the nadir of the correction from the April 2010 closing high, the DJIA had fallen 13.6% (closing basis). The losses were even worse in the S&P 500 and NASDAQ Comp., which dropped 16% and 17.3%, respectively.

With many prominent analysts and market pundits pounding the table declaring a new bear market was underway, Lowry's maintained the stance that the pullback, albeit painful, represented a correction within an ongoing primary uptrend. The reasoning behind this opinion was simple: Prior to the sell-off, there was a lack of evidence indicating a major top was at hand. This declaration was based on the same metrics observed during the decline from the January 2010 high.

Specifically, as was the case in January 2010, Selling Pressure did not experience a sustained uptrend heading into the April high. As already noted, there has never been a case in Lowry's history, which dates back to the early 1930s, where a bear market has begun with the Selling Pressure Index at its low. And at the April market highs, the downtrend in Selling Pressure dating back to the November 2008 peak remained intact, with the Index reaching a new low in its ongoing downtrend on April 23, one session prior to the peak in the Dow Jones Industrial Average (Figure 10.5). It is also clear in Figure 10.5 that Demand remained strong heading into the April high, given the uptrend in Buying Power.

In addition, the various A–D Lines monitored at Lowry's once again failed to indicate narrowing participation in the advance heading into the April top. The NYSE Composite all-issues, NYSE Operating Companies Only, S&P 500, S&P Mid Cap and NASDAQ Comp. A–D Lines all confirmed the new highs reached by their respective price indexes in the month of April. Figure 10.6 provides a look at the A–D Lines of the NYSE Comp. Index as well as NYSE Operating Company Only Index during this time period. Thus, while the market's tumble from the April high was significant, there was a lack of evidence suggesting investors should move to a heavily defensive position in anticipation of a forthcoming bear market.

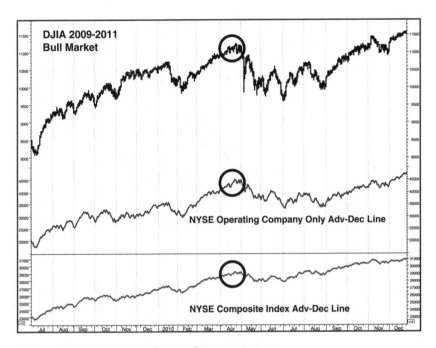

Charts created with Metastock, a Thomson Reuters product.

Figure 10.6   NYSE all-issues and operating company only A–D Lines

In early July 2010, worries about the market's broader trend were focused on what appeared to be a major topping pattern in the market, known in technical analysis jargon as a "head and shoulders top," as shown in Figure 10.7. A detailed description of the characteristics of this top can be found in any basic book on the subject of Technical Analysis or by just performing a Google search on the term. Some analysts were of the opinion that the price action from the top established in January 2010 through the breakdown below the late May/early June lows on June 30, 2010, represented a confirmed head and shoulders top. However, the forces of Supply and Demand were at odds with that opinion. Specifically, evidence of expanding Supply and contracting Demand was absent throughout the so-called topping formation. Had the formation of a major top been underway, eroding Demand should have been evident. To the contrary, Demand was expanding, with Buying Power rising from 150 at the start of the pattern in January 2010 to a level of 219 during the June 30, 2010, breakdown.

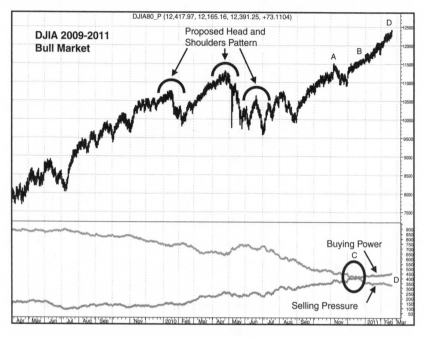

Charts created with Metastock, a Thomson Reuters product.

Figure 10.7   DJIA and proposed head and shoulders topping pattern

In addition, had a major top been in place, evidence of distribution should have been present. However, that was not the case, as Selling Pressure, after a reading at 752 in the early stages of the presumed head and shoulders pattern, was 32 points lower at 720 on June 30. In brief, measures of breadth (A–D Lines) and Supply and Demand all appeared to call into question whether the pattern actually represented a "classic" major topping formation.

Granted, using the Wyckoff methodology, the January 2010 high could have reasonably been labeled Preliminary Supply while the April peak could have been considered a potential major top. However, this example illustrates the importance of confirming elements such as the A–D Lines and measurements of Supply and Demand, all of which argued against the possibility a major top was at hand.

Indeed, the forces of Supply and Demand were proven reliable gauges of future market action as the late June break to new lows in the decline from the April high proved temporary and actually marked the low point of the correction. Subsequent gyrations in the weeks ahead were eventually resolved with an advance that surpassed the April rally peak in early November, as shown in Figure 10.7 (Point A). A modest pullback then developed throughout the rest of November, and by mid-December, the market, as represented by the Dow Jones Industrial Average (Point B), had recovered to new rally highs in its primary uptrend.

From that time through mid-February 2011, the equity market has been in the midst of a virtually uninterrupted move higher. This uptrend in equity prices is being confirmed by the actions of Supply and Demand, as Selling Pressure continues to steadily contract while Buying Power is in the midst of a persistent expansion. In fact, by December 20, 2010, Buying Power rose to a dominant position over Selling Pressure for the first time in three years, as shown by Point C.

History has shown that the amount of strength required to push Buying Power above Selling Pressure is often just about the same amount of strength required to push prices to a temporary over-bought level. Thus, market corrections often occur shortly after Buying Power/Selling Pressure crossing points. However, such was not the case this time as following the December 20 cross, the market continued its advance to higher highs within its primary uptrend, with the spread between Buying Power and Selling Pressure consistently widening, as shown by Point D.

As of mid-February 2011, the Dow Jones Industrial Average, S&P 500, NASDAQ Composite Index, New York Composite Index, S&P 400 Mid Cap Index and S&P 600 Small Index were all sitting at new highs in their respective primary uptrends dating back to the March 2009 bear market low. In fact, the S&P 400 Mid Cap Index is currently trading at a new all-time high. Also Buying Power and Selling Pressure are confirming the ongoing health of the primary uptrend, as the former is at a new rally high, and the latter is at a new reaction low, as shown in Figure 10.7. The various A–D Lines referenced previously in this chapter are providing confirmation of the of the bull market, as all are sitting at new rally highs. A final look at the A–D Lines of the NYSE Comp. Index and the NY Operating Company Only Index is shown in Figure 10.8.

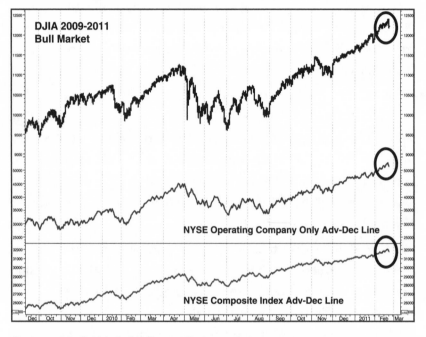

Charts created with Metastock, a Thomson Reuters product.

Figure 10.8   NYSE all-issues and operating company only A–D Lines

A final clue that neither the January 2010 nor the April 2010 top represented a major market high was provided by the application of Wyckoff's Law of Cause and Effect. This Law is applied through price projections for bull and bear markets through point and figure counts of major market tops and bottoms, as detailed in Chapter 6, "Building a Cause: How R.D. Wyckoff Uses Point and Figure Charts to Establish Price Targets." And the point and figure count for the 2008–2009 market bottom suggested the tops in January and April 2010 in the DJIA fell far short of the projected target range.

According to the Wyckoff method, the point and figure count for a market bottom is taken between two points, Preliminary Support and the Last Point of Support. The count represents the number of columns between those two points. Figure 10.9 of the DJIA uses the same three-box reversal method detailed in Chapter 6, with each box worth 100 points, also the same for the DJIA market tops and bottoms since 2000. As identified in the analysis of the 2009 market bottom in Chapter 5, "How Major Market Bottoms Form: Part II, Accumulation and Breakout," Preliminary Support is identified as the rally in mid-September to about 11,500 in the DJIA. The Last Point of Support is similarly identified as the early April pullback to around 7500.

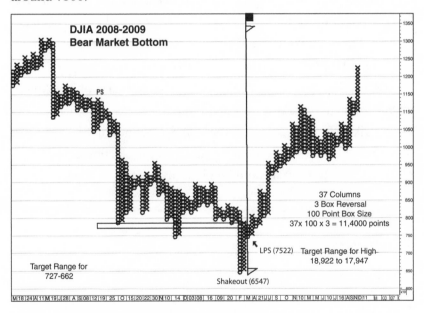

Charts created with Metastock, a Thomson Reuters product.

Figure 10.9   Point and figure chart of the DJIA: determining a potential target range for the Bull Market

The count is established by moving right to left along the level of this LPS to the column representing PS. This results in a count of 37 columns (boxes). The count is then finalized by multiplying the count (37) times the box size (100 points) times the reversal amount (3). Thus the count is 37 x 100 x 3 = 11,400 points.

This count is next used to establish the target range for the subsequent bull market and is projected from the level where the count originated (LPS) and also from the lowest point of the bottom formation, which in this case is the March 2009 market low. Adding the 11,400 count to the LPS at 7522 and to the March low 2009 at 6657 results in a target range of 17,947 to 18,922 for the current bull market in the Dow Jones Industrial Average.

As shown in the examples in Chapter 6, target ranges can sometimes be very accurate but other times not even close to the actual high of a bull market or low of a bear market. The ranges are used strictly as guides and potential benchmarks and are subordinate to other means of identifying market tops and bottoms. That said, the fact the target range for this bull market was so far above the January or April highs added another element to the evidence neither high was likely to represent a major market top.

The market has passed the two-year anniversary of the March 2009 bear market low. And given the evidence available from the intermediate-term trends of Supply and Demand, as well as from measures of market breadth and price target projections, the probabilities appear to favor a continued bull market in the months ahead.

Endnote

[1] See www.sec.gov/news/studies/2010/marketevents-report.pdf.

11

Putting It All Together

This book began with the statement, "Market timing doesn't work." Hopefully, the preceding pages have refuted that statement and indicated that, with the proper tools properly applied, market timing does work.

It is a contention of technical analysis that patterns and laws are fractal in nature. That is, a pattern that applies to the longer term will be equally applicable to the very short term, even on an intraday basis. That contention may give rise to differing opinions, but what does seem apparent is the reliability of these patterns increases in accordance with the period of time being analyzed. In other words, the probabilities of wrong timing is likely greater on a short-term basis when brief periods of market volatility can upset the most thorough analysis than when longer-term periods, such as the formation of major market tops and bottoms, is under examination. Thus, while the laws and analytical tools employed in this book appear effective when examining major events in the market, their application becomes progressively more difficult as the period under examination contracts. For example, small changes in an Advance–Decline Line or in measures of Supply and Demand are likely much less useful in analyzing the day-to-day movements in the stock market than the much more significant changes that accompany major moves in the market.

Because of their utility in measuring longer term market trends, the Wyckoff analysis, along with the Lowry analysis of Supply and Demand, seemed logical tools to use for identifying turning points in

193

major market trends. Although many years have passed since Wyckoff and Lowry developed their tools, the examples provided throughout this book indicate that, despite the changing world of the stock
market, human emotions remain the same throughout the various
stages of bull and bear markets. It is the consistency of human nature
that causes major tops and bottoms to show little change in their basic
characteristics over the years. This, in turn, makes it possible to successfully apply these methodologies to today's world of high frequency, computerized trading.

Bull and bear markets tend to represent significant events lasting
more than just a few months. Therefore, identifying when a major
trend is reaching its final stages can go a long way both in helping an
investor benefit from the upcoming major trend as well as preserve
the capital gains achieved during the preceding bull and bear markets. While not a precise formula, the steps in identifying a major
market top or bottom as outlined in this book tend to follow a similar
progression in successive bull and bear markets.

Typically, the first thing to look for as a warning market conditions
are becoming favorable for the formation of a major top is a deterioration in the NY Advance–Decline Line. This deterioration will also
likely be accompanied by a similar drop in the number of NY Stock
Exchange issues trading above their 30-week moving average. These
are the early warning signs that indicate investors should be alert for
the more timely indications a top is forming. The first such indication,
as outlined in previous chapters, is a sign of an unusual increase in selling, typically a rise in volume on a market pullback well above the volume seen on prior declines. This rise in volume is typically
accompanied by a rise in a measure of Supply, such as Lowry's Selling
Pressure Index.

The primary use of an indicator such as Selling Pressure is to
quantify the volume used in the Wyckoff analysis. It is rare that volume fits a neat pattern of smoothly increasing or decreasing on cue to
indicate expanding or contracting Supply or Demand. This is where

a longer term measure of Supply and Demand is most useful—in indicating the current trend in volume over and above the day to day fluctuations. Measurement of these trends is not limited to Buying Power and Selling Pressure. A simple moving average of volume or other measure of accumulation/distribution could be used. The important point is to find a means of quantifying the shifts in Supply and Demand to help identify the various points in a topping or bottoming process.

After identifying Preliminary Supply, the next point of reference should be the top itself, typically in the form of a Buying Climax or a process of churning in which consistent or rising volume fails to result in higher prices. The remainder of the analysis is in recognizing the various stages of the distribution process, culminating with a period of sharply falling prices on rising volume (or other measures of Supply), that breaks down to new lows (Breaking through the Ice).

The steps in identifying a major market bottom represent a progression similar to those needed to pinpoint a market top: An early warning (Preliminary Support, PS), a climactic event (Selling Climax, SC), and then various stages indicating Demand begins to dominate Supply. At the same time, there are certain tools useful in identifying market tops that have little application at market bottoms. For instance, while the NY Advance–Decline is a key indicator for identifying a market top, it is of little or no use for identifying a market bottom. The percent of NYSE issues trading above their 30-week moving average is slightly more useful and has given advance indications of an approaching market bottom in a few instances. But its record is too spotty to be regarded as reliable. Typically, the first sign of an approaching bottom is a rally on an unusual rise in volume (and increase in a measure of Demand), marking PS. However, probably the best indication of a market bottom is a SC.

Although up to 2007, 90% Days were rare at market tops, they were common at market bottoms and key in identifying SCs. Typically, a SC at a major market bottom will be preceded by one or more

90% Down Days, indicating the panic selling that precipitates the climax. These 90% Down Days are then followed by one or more 90% Up Days following the Selling Climax, indicating prices have been driven low enough to generate strong buying interest among investors—a necessary precondition for any new bull market.

Another key element in identifying a major market bottom is a steady withdrawal of Supply. This is typically indicated by increasing volume on rallies and decreasing volume on pullbacks as the bottoming process unfolds. However, just as in market tops, day-to-day volume is often volatile and seldom forms smooth rising or falling patterns. This is where measures of the trend in Supply become valuable, as they more clearly illustrate a pattern of contracting Supply as the bottoming process progresses, such as would be seen in a steadily declining Selling Pressure Index.

At some point, though, prices begin to move higher on rising volume (Buying Power) and move to new rally highs, signifying a breakout from the bottoming pattern, or in Wyckoff terms, a Jump Across the Creek. A successful test of the breakout (Backup to the Creek) typically signals the end of the bottoming process and the birth of a new bull market.

All this may seem cut and dried, but in fact, each market top and bottom is unique in how these patterns of shifting Supply and Demand play out. However, by studying the various market tops and bottoms discussed in this text, an investor can be armed with the tools needed to recognize these key turning points in the market's major trends. In so doing, we hope to have countered the contention that market timing doesn't work and provided investors with the means to reap the benefits of bull markets and weather the storms when bear markets arrive.

INDEX

Numbers